MW01231778

Tenure

Tenure

"How I Lived, Learned, Loved and Enjoyed a Long Successful Life"

Howard N. Hunter

Copyright © 2011 by Howard N. Hunter.

Library of Congress Control Number:		2011902893
ISBN:	Hardcover	978-1-4568-7305-9
	Softcover	978-1-4568-7304-2
	Ebook	978-1-4568-7306-6

All rights reserved. No part of this book may be reproduced or transmitted in any form or by any means, electronic or mechanical, including photocopying, recording, or by any information storage and retrieval system, without permission in writing from the copyright owner.

This book was printed in the United States of America.

To order additional copies of this book, contact:
Xlibris Corporation
1-888-795-4274
www.Xlibris.com
Orders@Xlibris.com
92601

Contents

DEDICATION

Benjamin Franklin said, "He who has a trade, has an estate." I dedicate *Tenure* to the memory of my loving grandmother, Sarah Darlington, in appreciation of her boundless love, inspiration, energy, and dedication to teaching me respect of God, my elders, and myself.

Acknowledgments

I GRATEFULLY ACKNOWLEDGE GOD for His Wisdom and Grace that allowed the following people to support, encourage, and assist me over the long walk of my lifetime including former and present students, friends, and co-workers, and to the following:

A very sincere and special gratitude goes to my dear friend Wanda Belgrave for many conversations, contemplations, and constant positive encouragement. Her hands-on expertise has been invaluable. Because of her, I have been able to transform my long desire to write my memoirs.

The Montford Point Marines I have met over the years filled in the missing blanks of African-Americans' early Marine Corps history in the United States. *Semper Fidelis!*

Katherine Chow, thank you for believing in me when no one else believe in me and for teaching me how to face the world on the world's terms. You will always be a treasure of my heart.

Hampden Engineer Equipment Control Division for encouragement in my early electrical teaching experience at Albert I Prince Technical High School in Connecticut.

Chapter One

A Miracle, Not A Mistake

I WAS BORN FOR a specific purpose. There! I said it. I am specifically designed to live and prosper in this dispensation of time. I have not always known my purpose but my grandmother, Sarah Darlington, identified it early and molded me accordingly. She taught me how to think soberly and to be self-controlled. Obedience to God was first, and self-respect was second.

My ability to lead young people to higher ground through lessons of right and wrong, or good and bad, were strict love lessons from Sarah. My minister once called me a "disciple among youth." I highly regard my ability to lead young people in a path of rightness to higher ground, teaching them to observe right and wrong. All that I am today I owe to God and my grandmother, Sarah Darlington.

I was supposed to be born Wednesday, June 18, but I already had a mind of my own. June 18 passed without incident. I chose June 30. On June 29 at 2:00 a.m., under a gorgeous, clear, beautiful southwestern breeze and an early morning Savannah sky, Larvesta, my birth mom, awoke to labor pains and called for my grandmother who was resting comfortably in the next room.

Her contractions were five minutes apart. As Larvesta walked the creaky wooden floor, Sarah dressed and started the forty-five-minute drive to the big city hospital.

Larvesta was a proud and reserved young lady. During the pregnancy when the subject of labor came up she'd say things like, "I will be the first woman to laugh and sleep through labor." She had a plan. She exercised, got plenty of rest, and drank plenty enough water. Obviously the voice of inexperience because when the labor started, so did Larvesta.

For the entire length of labor she screamed things like, "I can't do this" and "Make it stop!" From loud shrills her voice trailed to silent whispers as the pain mounted. I was ready to be born, and as this scenario would play out many times in my life, I was going to do it when I was good and ready. When Larvestas' words would not come she just grunted and moaned.

At the hospital, a midwife helped Larvesta into a warm tub of water. The contractions came harder and faster. With a towel wrapped around her neck, she patted Larvesta on her hand and said, "Only a little while longer now, dear."

Sarah sat on a stool nearby. Her legs twitched with every labor pain Larvesta experienced. Larvesta drew in a long breath, screamed, and heaved her full body out of the tub to a point like an Indian tepee and pleaded with Sarah to make the pain stop. When the midwife left the room, Sarah rolled Larvesta onto her right side and separated her legs in a scissorlike fashion. She leaned over and whispered in Larvestas' ear, "With this next contraction, push hard and give me this baby! Yah hear me?" Suddenly my chin was tucked into my chest and I was squeezed downward into a short dark tunnel. One contraction had not finished when another had began. With each push and shove I felt as if I was on a waterslide rocketing downward. Finally, a squeeze and a push with gazelle intensity I was determined to get through that dark, wet place and into the new world.

On June 30th, the world welcomed me, Howard Nathaniel Hunter, whose unparalleled determination and zest would help me conquer every task to be set before me.

In my life, I stared down racism, segregation, and overcame the limitations of polio and partial muscle paralysis, croup cough, swollen glands, fevers, and sore throat associated with diphtheria. I would walk first and walk again.

My grandmother had little reason from the doctors to hope for the best yet she hoped against hope. The doctors may have understood the diseases that plagued my body, but they underestimated the resolve of my loving grandmother. She would not be dissuaded where it concerned her baby boy.

I am told that Sarah stood under a Savannah Sycamore tree and prayed out loud to God as she declared greatness over my life. For sure there was much greatness to be had. She declared before God and man that not only would her baby boy walk up this world, but he would leave his mark everywhere he would trod. Sarah would be sure of that.

Sarah cut the umbilical cord and cleared mucus from my throat with her fingers. "Vesta!" she screamed. "It's a boy!" Her large arms were warm as a winter wool sweater. She massaged my back with long gentle strokes and swabbed my eyes with a warm moist towel. Our eyes smiled at each other. Leaning over Vesta Sarah chuckled and spoke softly, "His eyes are as blue as the Georgia Ocean." Her arms cradled my tiny body in a gentle caress.

Suddenly, I felt a heavy pressure in my chest. My eyes opened wide and the shunts in my heart closed. My lungs inflated like a balloon and I drew my first breath of life. There was a sweet aroma upon my inhale. It was one that I later associated with the smell of love, motherhood, and southern-baked sweet potato pie.

Swaddled tightly in a blanket, Sarah placed me on Larvesta's chest. This place seemed familiar, but I kept searching for the sweet aroma that first shaped my view of love. I was exhausted. Getting born had been hard work. It would prove to be the first mountain I would successfully climb. Being born to a mulatto mother and an African-American father was my second.

Some struggled with the circumstances and the consequences of my birth. I was sure that God had chosen every detail of who I was and who I was destined to become. I understood that He had endowed me with natural abilities, talents, and a specific personality. I was a physical manifestations of His mental creation. He appointed me to be here at this time. I was obedient and showed up.

I lived with a single mother and grandmother in a middle-class neighborhood in Can Park, Georgia, another mountain. I learned early to stand up for myself and for what I believed in. Fighting became a way of life. Literally, if I was going to live or going to have anything, I was going to have to fight.

The Ku Klux Klan was a violent white supremacy group. We were told how they burned down black churches, raped black women, terrorized, castrated, and hung black men in trees. There was no law that held this group accountable for their actions. There was no law for black people that white people were bound to respect.

For a group who disliked black people so much, they sure visited Can Park often to burn crosses on our lawns, drive fear into our hearts, and scorch our souls. It was a familiar sight to see children cower behind buildings and grown men hide under floorboards and in bottoms of potato bins in fear of their lives. This terror was a daily norm.

Black people were angry and resentful. As a young boy I realized I was powerless over this unfair treatment. I am still not sure if the trembling in my shoes was because I was more afraid, more angry, or both. But, it did not take me long to realize I had two choices. Accept it or die changing it.

Watching those people hiding under sheets with burning pieces of wood in their hands as they trampled Sarah's grass and gardens after months of sacrifice, planting, and hard work made my heart burn. But watching her cry as she picked up the pieces to start all over again was even more agonizing.

The die was cast. I was inclined to bring change to right this terrible wrong. My humble beginnings prepared me for the greater challenges I would ultimately face.

No matter how my life began I understood the full scope of it at a very early age. I was born at this time because I was necessary to this world and without my contributions, it could not be God's complete and wonderful creation. The only person who could make my contribution was me.

Each of us have a preordained purpose. If I don't do my part and you don't do your part, the world will be cheated out of our genius that will make it a better place.

Indeed, I have lived a challenging journey. I have done my best to leave the world a better place than I found it. This book is an attempt to share my story and encourage you to do your best on your life's journey as well.

Before I open this chapter of my life, I want to close another one by writing a letter to someone who is very dear to me. Without her, there would be no Howard. There would be no story.

HOWARD N. HUNTER

Dear Mother,

Words are too small to express what I believe your feelings must have been faced with the difficult decision to give up your baby boy. With limited choices you said you took the only available option. If I was going to have a fair chance at life you would have to place me with a loving and caring grandmother.

That choice forced memories that molded your thoughts of me. I know this because you told me, through salty tears, of the agony you felt as you watched me grow and play in Savannah.

You said you watched me drop the newspaper at your door, noting my knees peeking through my short pants and blowing in the wind as I peddled my blue and white bicycle. I was not just your son. I was your paperboy too. I have always wondered where you were, Mother. Why didn't you want me? Was I less lovable than your other children? You answered all those questions for me.

Meeting you was a fairy tale. Unbelievable! I look just like you. My smile was your smile. We walked and talked alike. I was your first child who grew under your heart and the first who drew breath from yours.

I am the son who spent a lifetime trying to make you proud. I would have traded it all for one moment with you. As you explained your pain I ached.

We scooped mutual love from a familiar place and time as we bonded a second time. I stared at you realizing God had exhaled and heaven was a very real place. Our hearts beat together without limits.

In that moment I realized that you were all the beauty I had dreamed of on parent nights, Mother's Day, birthdays, and graduations. I thought if I could imagine you were there I'd open my eyes and you would be there. I have always loved you mother and today I know you loved me too.

Joe gave me your picture. I carry it in my wallet. The real image of you I carry in my heart.

The years have conditioned me to the pain of your absence. Those memories share the space with your amazing presence. Sometimes I wonder if that day actually happened or if it was one of my perpetual childhood dreams. Today, my heart has the blessed assurance of your unconditional love for your baby boy. Mother, I pray that God blesses our shared love throughout eternity.

Your Blue-eyed Baby Boy, Howard

My birth mother - Larvesta

Chapter Two

The First Time I Saw Her Face

I DID NOT MEET my mother until I had entered the marines and was attending music school. While at music school, my captain requested me to the commanding officer of Battalion #1. When I reported, the first sergeant directed me to the Provost Office. He said, "Private, your mother wishes to see you!" I tried to explain to the sergeant that my grandmother had raised me and as far as I knew, my birth mother had died. "Private!" he snapped. "That is incorrect!" He gave me a seventy-two-hour pass and instructed me to go to the address on the paper he handed me and report back to him. "Orders complete!" he commanded.

Feeling shocked, confused and afraid, I stepped outside the Provost Office and the weight of my body fell against the closest wall. I remember thinking this can't be happening. But what was happening? That evening I packed and boarded the bus to Savannah the following day.

Arriving by taxi at the address on the small piece of paper I was still traumatized. Dressed in my summer uniform I knocked on the door. I was startled to see a very light-skinned woman who was as white as any white woman I had ever seen. Shocked and worried that I had knocked on the wrong door I apologized immediately and stepped away.

The woman with gray-streaked hair and large blue eyes stared at me as if she wanted to say something but I spoke first. "I am sorry," I said, glaring at the small piece of paper the Sergeant had given me. I continued, "I was sent to this address." I stumbled through the words. The lady grabbed me, cutting my words off hugging me as tight as a drum. I saw some little children playing in a room over her shoulder. They stared at me and I stared back. I was sure that I would be lynched for knocking on this white woman's door.

Again, I tried to pull from her embrace to explain that I had been sent to this address by my provost officer. She screamed in delight, "Junior? Junior? Oh my God! It's Junior? Is this you?" she squeezed me again. I thought she was not going to let me go and I was afraid that someone was going to see me in her embrace.

My experience with white women had not been positive. If someone was to see her hugging me I could be lynched or something. She pulled me into the house saying, "Come in" while throwing a barrage of questions at me. "Did you see big sister?" "No," I said, shaking my head side to side nervously, wondering who in the world was big sister. She pulled me closer hurling questions as if she could not believe what the answers could be. "Oh my God this is really you, Junior! Sit down. Sit down," she said, patting the seat of an old reupholstered wooden chair. "Wait until your uncle comes home. He will take us to see big sister." She stroked her hair back into a pony tail. I stared at her striking blue eyes. They looked just like mine.

I was shocked and confused. Everything was happening so fast. This had to be a dream. First, I am sent on a mission to locate someone whom I had long believed to be dead. Then, I arrive at the doorstep of a white looking woman who greeted me like she knew me, but I was sure I did not know her. Next, I saw several little very light-skinned kids playing in the next room.

I met my birth mother that evening. I first saw her out of the corner of my eyes and looked up just as she entered the room. It was a magical moment. The moment our eyes met my heart skipped a beat. I knew something incredible was happening and I instantly recognized her. She reminded me of someone I had known like an eternity ago.

Mother was wearing a simple multicolored one-piece cotton summer dress. Her hair was silky and jet-black, combed backward and sitting on her shoulder. She was not wearing any makeup. God knows she did not need any. This was too good to be true, yet it appeared that it was indeed very true. My lifelong personal struggle had come to a wonderful end.

We talked what seemed like endlessly. Actually, it was less than an hour. We talked as if we had always been best friends. For a moment I wanted to believe the past never happened, and that we had just met by mutual silent agreement. In fact, we were two halves of the same whole. Being near her seemed to be the cure I needed for the pain and emptiness that had afflicted me for so many years.

Caught in an emotion I had not experienced before, I stared at her. Every moment I stared at her, my feelings intensified. I was completely happy to see her for what I knew was "again." I felt the urge to hug her and wondered if she felt the same way.

I had always known there was someone else, a guardian angel or something bigger. I was aware of another loving presence but I dared not question my grandmother, Sarah Darlington. Furthermore, I was totally satisfied with Sarah as my mother. She was the only mother I would ever need.

My service at Parris Island Music School had been interesting but nothing would top the opportunity to meet my birth mother, encourage my young family members toward education, and help set standards for the development of their strong characters.

My brother had always been interested in the military and had grown up in the shadows of Hunter Air Force Base in Savannah. I encouraged him to enlist. He retired after thirty-one years as a Lieutenant Colonel.

On the long ride back to base something was happening to me. I became emotional as I filled in the missing pieces of the puzzle of my life. My mind questioned everything I thought I knew about myself, my life, my father and my grandmother.

The questions forced me to admit that all I thought I knew I really knew nothing. To make it worse things that once had confused me were making sense. I was an emotional wreck. I wanted to cry and laugh. I felt broken and complete at the same time. The trip helped me see possibilities for my life that I had not previously considered.

I had always felt another loving presence watching over me, but I dare not question my grandmother. When I was old enough to realize that Sarah was probably too old to be my mother I wondered about a lot of things. I knew that Sarah was the only mother I had and the only one I would ever need.

I had grown up a short distance away from there with my grandmother before we moved north to Connecticut. On the ride back, I noticed how the community had changed over time, but some things remained the same.

HOWARD N. HUNTER

There was the Catholic grammar school and the big corner church. Both suddenly seemed all too small. And the tree I used to sit under sometimes and skip rocks across the road looked a lot shorter to me.

I was glad that I met Larvesta. For the first time in my life I got to sit next to someone who looked like me. I was no longer the odd man out.

Meeting her made me more grateful to my grandmother. I realized that my life had been truly blessed over what it would have been living with a teen mom. I respect her for making that difficult decision to let my grandmother raise me. It turns out it was the right decision after all. With all of this new information I was a different man.

Chapter Three

Sarah Darlington

I AM BLESSED TO be the son of Sarah Darlington. She is the only mother I know and the only one I ever needed to know. She has been my greatest source of love and guidance for as long as I can remember.

Very early in life I learned that rules are followed to the letter in Sarah's house. I was going to be a leader, not a follower. Period. But to be a leader I had to learn to follow her leadership and that meant being obedient.

Obedience meant following instructions and we get along. Disobeying those instructions meant paying the consequences. I chose obedience. The decision would create a foundation for the development of excellent character.

To say Sarah was strict would be an understatement. Sarah was bold, brassy, and brave when she stood for something. She never took down off of anything she stood up for. Sarah was tough as rawhide outside, soft as a biscuit inside.

I am sensitive and empathetic to young people who are not fortunate as I to have had a loving woman like Sarah Darlington in their lives.

Sarah was the mistress of her own destiny and she instilled in me an unwavering personal resolve. She was committed to nothing less. I watched as she overcame difficult obstacles through courage and sheer will. She was grounded in strong morals, tough values, and a respect for life and she passed them onto me. I cherish them today.

The Male in Her Female

I refer to my grandmother often in these writings because I am the male in her female reflection. Through this personal connection I learned broadmindedness, sophistication, and tolerance. I learned to love children, animals, politics, reading, art, and responsibility. In her gentle composure I learned to be a *real* man because she was a *real* woman.

Sarah taught me everything and wasted no time making me understand God's commandments were serious business. Not to steal, kill or hold strife and jealousy toward others and to do so would cost me greatly. Because of these basic teachings my morals are rock solid and non-negotiable.

She was a gracious proud full-figured woman. Her skin was soft and beautifully tanned with high Indian height cheekbones and model-gorgeous, full, plump, and alluring lips. Often mistaken for a woman of Spanish descent, her race was not immediately obvious.

She was a principally centered mulatto woman of the prominent lineages of the early European, Indian, and African influences that crossed Savannah. Sarah was not a fancy dresser but she was a smart one. Earth tone colors flattered her figure. She had a bold quietness that outlined her brave confidence. She readily captured the attention of men. When she walked, she strutted square shouldered, challenging the world for her place in it. She was a stunning woman and a breath of fresh air.

Sarah loved children and was extremely successful at raising well-adjusted ones. She had three natural-born children: Mary, Martha, and Florence. Martha passed away before I was born. I grew up with Aunt Mary and Aunt Florence. They were successful women who left the south for opportunities up north in Connecticut.

Sarah had been a friend to my father's mother. When my paternal grandmother was dying she asked Sarah if she would take my father in so the white man would not make him a slave. Sarah did exactly that. She rescued the young lad and his brother, Julian, bringing them into her heart and making them part of her extended family. Later she welcomed my birth mother Larvesta and offered the young people a warm and loving environment.

Sarah was satisfied with her family, but, she had one problem. For years she had benefited from the old South's exclusionary laws and policies that profited whites in Savannah. Nonwhites were restricted from full participation in American society.

Sarah reasoned that if her young people and her blue-eyed baby boy would have a chance, she would have to break down the lines of racism that society had effectively locked them out of. She did, but she did it her way.

Although nonwhites, African-American's, Chinese, and Indians had no rights, any white man was bound to respect. The fact was they were taxed at the same rate but discriminated against made Sarah's blood boil. She longed to separate herself and her children from them.

Her Indian family members had become citizens through individual treaties and intermarriages. She used her Native American lineage to take a stand for the rights of Indians.

She fought the degrading Jim Crow housing laws that created redlining and effectively locked nonwhites out of buying homes just as many whites were getting in.

The Atlanta suburbs grew through a new majority class of whites. As programs helped qualify white communities for special benefits under the U.S. Census Act, minority communities were marked by urban poverty.

She knew if those disturbing discriminatory practices were to continue, they would protract our segregated communities and the substantial wealth between whites and nonwhites, giving whites further unfair access to wealth.

Sarah's Crow

Jim Crow laws flourished but Sarah had a crow in her own pocket. Sarah used her knowledge of these laws. She knew that the planners behind the initiative had labeled nonwhite neighborhoods "in decline."

The rules for loans did not say black families cannot qualify for the loans. It said people from areas in decline could not qualify. While the case could be made that the wording did not compel segregation, ultimately it had the same effect.

She used the laws and the color of her skin to purchase land in Can Park and rented the property to nonwhite land workers, small businessmen who otherwise could not qualify to rent or afford to buy such property.

She knew also that centuries of inequality would not be remedied overnight and color-tainted policies would continue to perpetrate disparities. She did the next best thing to ensure this blue-eyed baby boy would be guaranteed a fair shake in life. Sarah had a plan.

Rosa Parks Sat Sarah Darlington Stood!

Before Rosa Parks refused to give up her seat to a white passenger on a bus; before the NAACP coined the phrase, "Equal but separate" (Brown v Education); Sarah Darlington pioneered her way through segregation using the only weapon she had—the color of her skin.

At the time of Sarah's death in 1942, she had not realized the results of her fight nor the new nondiscrimination her actions would help to bring about. That would not come until the late sixties or early seventies when civil rights protests stood against segregation.

Sarah lived through the southern white attitudes curse of ignorance that denied children the rights to an education. By the time whites decided to allow nonwhites to attend school she had already been reading with an oil lamp at night.

She believed in education, especially mine, and would stand for nothing in the way of it. She was my personal educational advocate and coach. At St. Mary's Elementary School in Savannah I was bound to excel. She would stand for nothing less.

Sarah had a pure heart and a simple love for God's people. She'd say, "Love God, son. Try to do the right thing and God will take care of the rest." She believed that and I came to believe it too.

A Good Cook

Sarah was always in her kitchen. Anyone who was not a good cook could not get close to her kitchen. She said she learned her cooking skills from the old folks during slavery. However she learned it, she knew it well. She could really cook.

My grandmother never had to wake me for breakfast. I was summoned by the downwind smell of Mama's mouthwatering sugar-cured bacon and ham, homemade biscuits with creamy butter, and fresh sap from Auntie's kindling maple tree out back.

I always knew dinner was cooking when I smelled Uncle T's fresh caught catfish in Mama's special catfish head soup with fresh onions, garlic, celery, and spices and her way down south red beans and rice with collard greens and pig's feet. I used to hurt myself eating at her dinner table. The potbellied round black cast-iron stove added coziness to the house. Breakfast was cooked on two burners out front and dinner at the back.

They told us that old people ate chicken feet because the collagen in them prevented wrinkles, but they really ate them because often there was nothing else to eat. The plantation owners threw these parts of the chicken away. The slaves gathered, cleaned, cooked and served them to their families for dinner

I understand why these foods were discarded, but as black people we had no choice. We ate that or nothing. We made do with what we had and we gave thanks for it.

Before dinner was on the table, my hands were washed, blessings prayed, and I was eating by six o'clock every night. I couldn't wait!

Sunday guests added zest to our table. Fried chicken was a Sunday dinner staple. I watched from a half-shut eye during the blessing to see if a guest would leave a chicken leg. They never left a leg; sometimes a wing, but never a leg. I secretly swore that at my kitchen dinner table I would always get the chicken leg.

We dined on soul food at its best but Sunday always included black-eye peas and sweet potato pie, fresh apple pie with apples from our orchard, or blackberry pudding.

There was little waste. Adding egg, corn meal, and seasonings turned leftover fish into croquettes for Monday's breakfast. Add raisins and sugar to stale bread and it became bread pudding. The liquid from the turnip greens became a pot liquor drink. Breakfast was all set. As a growing boy I could not sleep fast enough.

Family Chats

When everyone was too full to do anything else we'd loosen our belts and move to the front porch. Family time automatically followed the evening meal. The children gathered for stories and games. The elders caught up on weekly gossip and told us all about ourselves.

During these times we learned about the greatness of our grandparents and family members. It seemed that every time someone new told the same story, we learned more and more. It was more dogs shot under that Talbot tree. That fish that Grandpa James caught grew longer every year, and it was always longer than the newest baby born in the family.

We learned that we were born of African kings and queens. That there were black men and women in the Bible and they were some of the great men we'd studied in Sunday school.

They told us that Africa was a huge continent. Her people were smart, educated philosophers and astrologers. They never spoke in broken languages or swung in trees like Tarzan and Jane on television.

In fact, they said Africans and ancient Egyptians created languages with hieroglyphics. Hieroglyphics were used as a written language. Each of the symbols stood for a sound. Unlike English, hieroglyphics were used phonetically. Over the centuries there had been many spectacular cultures with their own unique symbols and alphabets but none as spectacular as the Egyptians with their hieroglyphics. No one actually swung in trees like Tarzan on television. They told us that back in the day, black men were scientists, explorers, and inventors.

A guy named Matthew Henson was a black explorer who explored with Admiral Peary. Peary became very sick on the last journey and could not complete the trip to the north pole. He sent his buddy, Matthew Henson, to complete the journey for him. Henson was the first black man to reach the North Pole and planted the American flag. Because of Mr. Hensons heroic measures the United States is credited with being first to reach the North Pole. Admiral Peary was awarded many honors. Matthew Henson was largely ignored.

William Purvis improved and patented a fountain pen like the one we used in school. He also invented two machines for making paper bags and sold the patents to the Union Paper Bag Company of New York.

John Stannard patented designs for improved refrigerators and oil stoves. Garrett Morgan invented a traffic signal like the one on the corner of our house. They told us that he made national news for using his gas mask to rescue thirty-two men trapped during an explosion in an underground tunnel two hundred and fifty feet beneath Lake Erie. We thought that was so cool.

Auntie said the first black man to patent anything was a man named Thomas Jennings in 1821, patenting a dry-cleaning process called

Dry Scouring. They would talk for hours about the greatness of black people. They even told us that black slaves helped build the United States White House. In fact, they said, there is proof to this account in old information sources of Washington, DC. I don't know if I really believed it but I guessed it could be true.

We were excited and wanted to believe every word. I said if this stuff is true, why was it not in our history books like other peoples' inventions? The only thing we ever heard about was a guy named Eli Whitney who invented a cotton gin to pull cotton faster and a man named Thomas Edison and the light bulb. I was curious about a white man who designed a machine that would make it easier for black people to pull cotton since he never had his fingers torn apart by the thorns. Why would he care?

Overall, I was convinced that they were real black people who had inventions but couldn't own them as property or get any money because they themselves were slaves and the property of their slave masters. Only the slave masters could benefit from the inventions of these smart black people. These slaves would never see much if any of the royalties for thier inventions.

There were stories of racism like when Uncle Joe was hung in the old Sycamore tree by six white men who were out for a good time that evening.
They told us how his manhood had been cut from his body and stuffed in his mouth while he remained defenseless with his hands tied behind his back. The cigarette burns on his buttocks, back and legs had been carefully placed in perfect circular patterns as if it was the result of some weird sadistic game.

His shirt was stuck to open cross cuts made by tree limbs, switches, leather belts and belt buckles. His captives had made a contest or game out of who could make the deepest gash on his black skin. The tally of the game was found on the ground under his body. They instructed us to look for the hang notches on the trees when we passed on the way to school.

As bad as that was, they hung him on a tree down the road from where he lived. His mother would be sure to discover him hanging there. No one was ever brought to justice for these ridiculous crimes against humanity and black people.

HOWARD N. HUNTER

My uncles told of stories when they were chased by white men like animals and beaten with sticks, run under houses and behind trees just because someone, usually a white, did not like the way they looked.

The pain on their faces is forever etched in my memory as they told us how they cut him down from the slave tree and the awful thud sound his body made when he hit that hard ground. These stories were told with empathy and in quiet whispers as if they were afraid someone would over hear them and they may be next.

With wide eyes and open ears we huddled closely wondering if something like that could happen to us. These stories are my earliest recollections of decent good strong wise black people who set the standards by which we were to measure ourselves.

In these family gatherings we learned everything good about ourselves. No one else ever told us anything good about ourselves or that our family members were champions or inventors. In fact, our family members were champions with impeccable character who had been unfairly treated by a racist society. Each of us pledged to never forget them and not let their lives have been lived in vain. Their memories are forever frozen in our memories.

I asked if we could claim some of that money from those inventions since we were not slaves anymore. Hurriedly, auntie rushed to my side and whispered, "Hush, chil, talkin' like det! You'd louda be necks!" or "G'woin way from here, chil, shush your moud. Let some white person here yah talk like dat you louda be next!" But I was angry and I wanted to reclaim what was rightfully mine. Uncle Joe would lean forward in that creaky rocking chair, look in my eyes, and softly repeat something he told us all of the time, "Dey sayed weed beez free, but weez aint free, not really."

I am not sure how much was told us was believed by the other children but I believed every single word. I'll admit it was hard to believe that God talked to black people in the Bible but I guess it could have happened. I guess.

Chapter Four

The Preacher Comes to Dinner

THE PREACHER HAD a standing invitation to Sarah's dinner table. Sometimes he had many Sunday dinner invitations. This guy could put some food away. He could really eat. Where did he put it all? He said he visited Sarah's table first so he could eat a belly full of good food, and for her homemade sweet potato pie and potato salad, then he'd visit others. I think he would have eaten a belly full no matter where he went first.

Sarah enjoyed his presence for it seemed to confirm a degree of prestige in the eyes of the rest of the congregation. It made Sarah smile but I wondered if he told everyone the same thing.

Sarah was a proud Christian woman. Before dawn on Sunday morning and before the cocks could get the spiders out of their eyes we were off to the First African Baptist Church.

One of our after dinner stories was told by the preacher himself. It was the story of how many years ago the church had been called the First Bryan Baptist Church but the blacks and whites couldn't get along and the congregation split. From that point forward blacks and whites worshipped separately.

He said that the church was the oldest African-American church in North America. I wasn't quite sure where North America was at that time but I was very proud to be a part of it.

He told us that the church began changing the lives of young people in Savannah a very long time ago. It changed mine and I am very happy to have been a member in the early days. Its legacy continues today with self-esteem awareness and youth entrepreneurial programs, a credit union, and a business center that encourages social and economic stability in the community.

Food and friends are, and have always been, the glue of our extended families. Everyone was welcome and everyone was considered family. My grandmother taught me that if there was room in the heart, there was room in the cart. When families got together, it was to nurture the young familial relationships. Food was always a part of fellowship. It held us together in difficult times.

My grandmother went out of her way to bring family and friends together and to make our family gatherings memorable. There was not a lot of money and no special preparation but once assembled each gathering was a very special experience.

It was not unusual to borrow a cup of flour or a cup of sugar from a neighbor to complete a meal and of course everyone could just drop by for a meal. There was no shame, just a willingness to help each other.

We wore hand-me-down dungarees and passed our gently used ones on to the next smallest kid in the community. Sarah told me something did not have to be new to be good. She was right. No one ever laughed when we saw the kid down the street with our old dungarees. We were just happy to help.

We can do that today. We can align our family schedules for simple picnics, Sunday dinners, and softball games. All types of reunions can be deeply satisfying for everyone. When families get together, children remember the fun and good times. They develop a sense of who they are and from where they come. We can again create a welcome atmosphere of love in our homes for our families. Can we create opportunities where children can form positive opinions that open their hearts to others?

All families are different and some of us have allowed small problems to grow into serious evils. Many of us are emotionally damaged due to some relationships. Some wounds are deep. These families are not unique.

We had problems back in the day. Some of today's problems stem from yesterday's bitterness. But if we are going to save our children, future generations, and the notion of family, we must fix the strained relationships that have destroyed our family. Relationships that cannot be fixed must be lived with.

Chapter Five

Aunt Laura
A Special Kind of Love

WHEN I WAS about five years old, my grandmother took in a small frail crippled woman. I knew her only as Aunt Laura. Sarah was very kind to aunt Laura, feeding her proper meals and medication. Sarah always loved cooking for the elderly in the Old Folks Home. Aunt Laura was an extension of her love for the people who needed help.

Aunt Laura's knuckles and joints were twisted with arthritis and gnarled with pain. She only used her hands when she was forced too. The gentle wrinkles forming in her face contoured on a grimace each time she moved her fingers.

Despite Aunt Laura's illness she was a brilliant quick-thinking woman. She sat quietly for long hours looking out of the large picture window on the east side of her bedroom. I was a mischievous lad who enjoyed peeking at her. I always wondered what she must be thinking.

Sarah was blessed with many talents. She could have been a doctor too. She had a homemade remedy for everything and it grew in her garden out by the fence. Through Sarah's strange healing powers Aunt Laura eventually walked and at a smart pace even in the morning when her legs hurt her the most.

Sarah had learned an old-fashioned Indian and African oil massage technique. She used a mixture of what felt like gravel and fruit seeds. It smelled like a mixture of fresh released skunk and horse manure. It smelled awful!

Sarah would have Aunt Laura close her eyes and place her hands in a chipped large white resin ceramic bowl. She would put Epsom salt in the bowl and pour warm tap water over her hands. "Just rest, Laura, so you can get better," she'd say and begin gently stroking her hands. She'd begin a ritual of massage. The heels of her hands and her wrist became a mortar while stretching Aunt Laura's fingers far apart—touching the left fingers to the right palm and the right fingers to the left palm rotating both thumbs in circular motions. Like magic, aunt Laura would stretch her fingers far apart.

After ten minutes or so she'd paint both hands with some fishy-smelling liniments. That room was always serene. Only the sound of swishing slow-moving water filled the eerie quiet. Aunt Laura smiled at Sarah as if to show appreciation.

Aunt Laura was even more grateful to my grandmother when she was able to move her hands without pain. Over time Aunt Laura's hands looked smooth and soft as the white ladys' hands on that Jerkins hand lotion commercial. Aunt Laura and Sarah eventually became the best of friends.

Aunt Laura could read and write very well. She was a shrewd negotiator and a smart business woman. She became Sarah's personal secretary for her entrepreneurial projects.

My grandmother recognized a teaching moment when she saw one. Taking Aunt Laura in was just such a moment. She reminded me that as long as I was healthy, I had an obligation to stay that way so I could help those less fortunate than I. According to Sarah Darlington, there were many people less fortunate than I. She said if I could not help someone I had better not hinder thier progress.

At the supermarket, my grandmother added her dime to President Franklin Roosevelt's March of Dimes initiative to find a cure for polio. She was passionate and personally motivated. I had been a polio survivor during the days of iron lungs, hydrotherapy baths, and when children wore leg braces. The public swimming pools closed in those days because of polio scares.

Sarah had suffered the anguish of nursing me back from the ravages of that dreaded disease, but, she never allowed me to use that illness as an excuse. She reminded me daily that two million other children were struggling with the same disease. Sarah was a "no nonsense, no matter what" person and she spoke it into my life saying, "Howard, with God's help you *will* walk!"

Sarah knew that if a person with a healthy and perfect body could be discriminated against because of the color of their skin, Aunt

Laura's problems in society would be much worse. She thought it her job to help Aunt Laura reach her full personal greatness.

When Aunt Laura moved into our house she moved into our hearts and it was not long before she became part of our extended family. She enveloped our family in her uncompromising love too. She has had a huge influence on the person I am today. It wasn't blood ties but it was kinship ties.

There are many lovely things about Aunt Laura. She wove a non-materialistic tapestry of love throughout our family. We shared long hours telling stories and jokes from her family's past. She gave me a feeling of permanence and a sense of history that has supported me during hard times.

Sarah made Christmas and birthdays happen. Aunt Laura made them magical. She made homemade cookies and baked her special melt-in-your-mouth pound cake. She guided me through the school system supporting and loving me at every angle. This may be old-fashioned, but it was love and it lives in me today. There are still things in my memory that shaped my life way back then. Everyone does not have to be blood to be family. Family begins at the point where you make a love connection.

Cleanliness Is Next to Godliness

Aunt Laura, like the rest of the family, had pretty milky white sheets. Weekly Sarah filled her round number two steel wash basin with warm water from the wood potbelly stove. She scrubbed our clothes with a large square bar of homemade goat milk soap. She loosened the dirt with a large stick, washed, rinsed, and hung them out to dry on the front porch. If it rained, we dried them in the dining room. In the winter, we freeze dried them on the clothesline outside. It didn't usually get that cold in Savannah, though. Whatever the circumstances, Aunt Laura had the whitest lemony fresh-smelling sheets.

"Mama," I asked, "how do you get those sheets so white?" In the warm morning breeze her shining gray hair danced effortlessly over her shoulders as the sun reflected through it. Her pink wash dress blew backward and forward held together by two large buttons at her waist. It had two very large pockets that fed her a continuous stream of old-fashioned wooden clothespins.

She flashed me her winning smile that is permanently etched in my mind. "Son," she said, "I've got a secret." Secret? Mama tell me, tell me!" I said, smiling up at her with my missing tooth grin and those big blue eyes. She loved my blue eyes and with them I could usually get anything I wanted from her. Not this time. "I won't tell you," she said.

"But I like secrets too" I said as I circled her long legs going around and around her like the peppermint stick on the barbershop pole. She interrupted, "If I tell you, it will no longer be my secret." I giggled. She smiled and rubbed the top of my head, pushing a falling clothespin back into her large dress pocket with her other hand. She never told me the secret but I think I figured it out.

The next wash day while hiding behind Aunt Laura's door, I watched grandmother prepare the wash. She pretended she did not know I was watching her. But if it is one thing I know about my grandmother I could get nothing past her. She knew I was there.

A dash of hydrogen peroxide, a pinch of baking soda, a cup of white vinegar, and the juice of a full lemon was her secret. Aha! No wonder the sheets smelled like fresh lemons. My grandmother was so smart. Clorox bleach costs ten cents a jigger but she could buy these special ingredients at the general store for only a nickel and use them to wash and cook. Most of them she used in the kitchen too. Sarah no longer had a secret because I knew her secret and when this wide eyed curly-headed little boy knew a secret, it was no longer a secret. I was like a Savannah telegram. I was going to tell the world.

Chapter Six

Mr. Jake
A Good & Honorable Man

MR. JAKE WAS a handy man. This guy knew his stuff and he knew all the rules as they applied to black people. Slaves could not walk around freely although they were not supposed to be slaves anymore. They had no real family or had been separated through slave "tree" sales. Some had been studded to other white slave owners for the purpose of making strong, healthy slaves to eventually work the plantations. Whatever the case, after a few generations of studding black men and selling slave babies no one was sure who their kin was anymore. Therefore, slaves began to refer to each other as brothers and sisters. This is still true today. The truth is there is just no way to trace our true family ancestry without running into multiple slave owners and facing diversions.

Slaves ate what they could eat when they could get it, and they ate it when they were told. There were no jobs available for slaves other than working the plantations from which they had been supposedly freed. Some ended up returning to the house and field slave jobs working for their old slave masters. Most had significant life skills they had learned like, planting, harvesting, cooking or babysitting. They were not educated though and no one was going to hire them.

They had no human rights and nothing was going to get better unless they made it better for themselves. They would have to go into business for themselves and try to sell their goods and wares to previous slave owners.

Mr. Jake was used to hard work. He had worked on plantations since he was a boy with sixteen to twenty-four hour workdays including three months planting and harvest seasons from sun up to sun down.

He was a tall, dapper, clean-shaven man who wore a bowler hat with a wide brim. He always wore a serious inquisitive look as if he was always trying to figure something out. He had a weird habit of sitting in a folding wooden chair sideways with his long legs crossed and swinging.

He dreamed of running his own lumber company. Sarah thought he deserved a chance to do that. As he had little to start, Sarah reached into her pocket and pulled out an opportunity. She rented him a space on her land at a minimum price and loaned him money to get started. That was my grandmother. With her help and his skills he became a successful minority business owner in Savannah. Whenever we ate dinner, she made a plate of food for Mr. Jake and gave it to me to deliver to him. Sometimes she invited him inside for a meal with the family.

Sarah taught me to be generous through her own generosity. She taught me that Christianity in a building on Sunday morning or in a prayer on my knees was just the beginning. She said Christianity was really what you do when you leave the building and get up off of your knees from praying. In fact, love is an action she said, not just a word. I learned that I was not a Christian until I have put love into action. The best love, she said, was charity from my heart.

On occasion I heard Mr. Jake moving lumber around the yard and dropping his tools. One day he wept as he told my grandmother how grateful he was for all she had done to help him claim his life. She told him to do the same for someone else. He vowed he would do that. Sarah believed in paying love forward. She did it all of the time. I admired Mr. Jake's sacrifice and determination.

There was another man who was disabled and blind. He rented the front cottage from Sarah. I was very young and do not remember his name. He too, was a proud, stately man. I heard my grandmother whisper that he had been a runaway slave from Mr. Charleys' place up yonder. One day one of massas head hunters caught him reading by candlelight and ran and told massa Charley. The next day massa Charley took him out back to the slave shed, called his house and field slaves to watch as he poured acid into the man's eyes. They watched as his eyeballs literally boiled out of his head and rolled onto the ground. He warned the other slaves that this is what would happen to them if they ever tried to learn how to read or run away from his plantation. They were afraid and they did not doubt him. They had witnessed run-away slaves having their feet cut off many times before. Once Massa Charley caught a house slave giving left over bread crumbs to the field slaves and cut three of her fingers off of each hand. He said she was stealing from him.

Every day for as long as I can remember, I had to take food to this mans' house, remove his garbage, or see if I could help him in any way. He called me Little Howard. He would chuckle my name, run his hand through my curly locks of hair, put two starlight mints in my dungarees pocket and admonish me to be a good boy. He was like a very kind uncle.

There was never a person my grandmother did not help if she thought she could. She was a strong asset to her family and a great contributor to her community. She was an intellectual woman of purpose always involved in productive activities. Above all, she was God-fearing. I was so blessed to have her call me son.

America's Generational Shame

I speak to children who are carrying burdens of old family members who died leaving their fights unfinished. Their children carry these old grudges and are fighting battles so old they no longer know why they are fighting. Most only know that Mother was fighting with someone and believe it is their duty to continue the anger and to pass it on to the next generation. If you ask them why they are fighting with so and so they cannot tell you. They do not know.

Others are not speaking with family members because they remember when Daddy was not speaking to them. This is our generational shame passed onto our children. That is very sad. We are doing our children a grave injustice when we burden them with old unresolved problems. We must allow the children to love family and grow close to extended family without biases.

It is our responsibility to set aside old grievances and encourage our children to love completely and fully through family memories. We can do this. We can heal our families starting with ourselves. We can begin by organizing small reunions inviting those who are ready and want to attend. We can hold the money spent on presents or unnecessarily at the holidays and go to visit family members instead.

We can get together, take a walk, play parlor games, or just talk about good old times. We can listen. We can and must forgive.

We can plan to have just a good time. It is what Sarah taught me by providing Sunday dinner and after dinner chats. If we are going to save our children and therefore our future, we have no choice. We must start right where we are. We must start today.

Chapter Seven

The Old Folks' Home

EVERY THURSDAY I had a job because my grandmother had a job. She cooked for the people in the Old Folks Home uptown. My responsibility was to load my little red wagon with the home-baked goodies and deliver them to the people who lived there.

Sarah was diligent to the vulnerable people at that Old Folks Home. She just loved them and seemed like she got a personal gratification from giving her time, cooking and organizing those meals for me to deliver to them. She acted as if she had been called by God to do it. Maybe she was.

That Old Folks Home was nothing less than warehousing facilities for the aged and helpless that society labeled undesirable and worthless. Sarah had great respect for the elderly and she taught me to do the same. She'd say, "Son, without them, there would be no us. We must respect them and all they have done to leave us a better world than they had lived in." I learned to respect that early.

She loved the tenth commandment in the Holy Bible, "Honor your father and mother." I dare not give off an I-don't-want-to-do-this attitude. I'd better act like I liked it even if I didn't. But, actually I did like it.

In reality, that Old Folks Home was just a crime against humanity. It reminded me of the dark ages with a tall shadowy gothic gray rundown wood frame structure that seemed to sway in the high Savannah winds.

The grounds were not well kept. Weeds, shrubs, and trees grew wildly across the doors and windows. Day-old newspapers sprinkled the fifteen-step incline. The long broken cemented driveway was simply a means of connecting the house and the public access road. The linoleums inside the building buckled from the overflow of water that leaked through the roof.

Tiny rooms separated society's discarded men from the women. Awful squeals of discontented residents shrieked in the halls. Injuries, falls, black and blue marks, broken hips, and bedsores were all obvious signs of elder abuse.

Visitors and family members treated this situation as though it was normal. It was very stressful and life changing for me. I swore that no matter what happened to me in life, I would work to never have to be dependent upon such a place. And no matter what it would take, I would never live or die unloved, lost, or forgotten. This was a terrible way to live or die. That experience motivates me to stay healthy, watch my diet, and live a clean life.

The attitude of the white people who scowled at us at the door was as powerful as the smell that blew past them when they opened it. A fishy, ammonia stench of urine and rotten feces overpowered us. We covered our noses with our shirts as we eased inside.

As awful as this place appeared, it was probably the only place where black and white people lived together in Savannah. At this Old folks home color wasn't the discrimination of choice—age was. You just had to get old, be classified as society's waste, and you could live there. That's all. And it did not matter the color of your skin.

These poor people had seen better times. Life's twists and turns had landed them in this sanitarium to live out their last days. Their eyes were the windows of their souls. Weakened strengths showed grueling shadows of lost loves. Gray eyelashes swept puddles of missed opportunities from their eyes.

This wide-eyed boy with a burning desire to right "wrongs" and change the world wondered about this concentration camp of tortured old people. I wondered what if anything could be done for these poor lost souls.

Before foods were dated, unsafe food practices were the norm. Chemical and manmade contaminates, nutritional deficiencies, and old moldy food caused many diseases and premature death. Food poisoning was not uncommon.

My grandmother would not let me come inside the house, have a drink of water and I had better not ask for anything to eat before washing my hands. She said keeping my hands clean was the best thing I could do to keep down the spread of germs. I don't ever recall seeing residents or employees of that Old Folks Home wash their hands.

Mean looking nurses in bleached white uniforms carried medication around in large empty animal feed buckets like the ones we used to feed the hogs or to lay sod in the garden. It seemed that no matter what the illness, everyone received the same pink and white pills from that bucket. Some received two pink and white pills. Memories of rotten food being forced into their digestive systems still haunt me.

In recent times the homes have changed for the better. They are no longer called Old Folks Home, rather nice names like Nursing Homes, Assisted Living Facilities or Homes for the Aged. These names give the impression of "purity" where elderly people are really cared for. "Saturday Night Fever" and disco dancing were also introduced to the daily routine. This gave the illusion that the homes had become a place to "assist the elderly" in living their lives out more richly.

Facility tours highlight new kitchens and recreation rooms. Activities included picnics, movie nights, and social outings. Resident rights programs in some states must allow residents "private" time. From their descriptions you can smell home-baked gingerbread cookies and envision a life of luxury for your loved one.

Sarah's Salvation

My grandmother gave me a gift when she made me passionate about the needs of the elderly. I have gained so much pride from this life's experience. I will never forget the long trips to that home delivering what I came to call Sarah's Salvation for those poor people.

Today, this phenomenon is a national tragedy. Those who choose to not share love with the elderly are missing a life education that they could get nowhere else. Our elderly are golden nuggets of knowledge from a time long ago. They've got stories and funny jokes. They remember what your town looked like before you were ever born. Imagine that.

Families who drop off their precious elderly at the door of such places and fail to return miss a lifetime of fulfilling personal relationships. This leaves the elderly filled with righteous indignation and causes them to close the door on their lives earlier than they would if they believed someone loved and cared for them.

This grave injustice is also pervasive in many veterans' homes across this nation today. Many men and women at the veteran's homes are more than heroes. Many of them are Medal of Honor recipients. All have sacrificed their lives, many their limbs and others their personal freedoms for this country. It is a national disgrace to recognize that many of their hired caretakers have little more than a high school diploma or basic nursing assistance certificates. Others are under correctional supervision for crimes against the elderly including elder abuse. For many, taking care of our precious elderly is just another job that pays the bills. I believe that people who work with this population should be specially trained to meet the delicate requirements and needs of this irreplaceable population of great men and women. Afterall, they gave society their best.

When I visit with our veterans, we talk about the olden days and what happened in their lives. We reflect on their families. I make it a habit to bring memories such as hard rock candy that was popular back in their day. Some just want a slice of sweet potato pie or old-fashioned peppermint sticks. These small tokens remind them of home and better times.

Sarah loved the tenth commandment to honor your father and mother that your days may be long upon the land that God gave you. That commandment was the only one with a promise attached: honor your parents and live long, dishonor your parents and die early, simple.

I wonder if there could be a connection to this commandment with the increased numbers of young people dying so young. If they respected this commandment, might they live stronger, healthier, longer lives?

Manifest Your Own Destiny

This life lesson helped me realize that if I did not want to leave my later life experiences to chance, I had better manifest my own destiny and I had better do it early. You should do it too.

Choose to live the good life outside of what society determines is successful for you. Your success is a personal matter. Incorporate an internal sense of accomplishment and satisfaction. This is your work and I guarantee you it will not come easily. You must set your own standards and exceed them. This will be your personal success in life story. Here are some of the dos and don'ts I have learned to live by. They may help you too.

- Don't let life catch you out of self-control.
- Always be in control of yourself and your actions
- Don't let others influence you unless it is what you want to do.
- Set achievable goals. This is the most reliable method to identify what you want to achieve. Your goals should not be written in stone or inflexible so you can adjust them from time to time.
- Be yourself. Don't try to be good at something you do not enjoy doing.
- Strive for what you want and don't be easily discouraged.

For one reason or another, many of the people in that Old Folks Home never discovered their full capabilities. They never dared to dream to be anything other than what others wanted them to be. Too often, they gave up for too few reasons. Something was difficult. They were lazy. They lacked a belief in themselves or their abilities. Every excuse will be addressed when you value your own life and something greater than yourself. Try it.

Once I made a commitment to my personal success. Impossibilities became challenges to overcome and I resolved them under a personal focus on who I wanted to become.

Chapter Eight

Non-negotiable Respect

AS A TEACHER in a public school system, I recognize that respect for adults have faded and often no longer exists. Children are not naturally inclined to respect their elders. They must be taught and experience role models of respect.

My grandmother required me to respect others. This was not negotiable when it came to any elders, adults, parents, teachers, neighbors, and anyone she determined had rule over me.

I grew up during a time when children were taught manners and expected to follow them without exception. We could not interrupt an adult conversation or differ with an adult. We did not have enough experience as an adult (none really), to correct anything an adult said.

On the street, women passing on the sidewalk were greeted by men who stepped aside to let them pass. If they were smoking, they quickly removed that cigarette or cigar and said, "good morning" or "good evening."

Men never wore hats inside of a building. Hats were removed upon entering a building. Women were allowed to wear a head covering under certain conditions.

No child ever entertained the thought of calling an adult by their first names. In fact, every adult was Miss, Mr. or Mrs. We answered an adult question with "yes," "no," "no thank you" and requested something with polite words as "please," "may I have," and "thank you."

At our dinner table, it was not unusual for children to wait until our mothers had taken the first bite of food before we could begin eating or wait for their permission to begin. Someone at that table was going to offer a prayer of gratitude and thanksgiving or no one was going to eat. We knew when respect was due and we honored it.

There would be no one sitting during the Pledge of Allegiance. Pledging allegiance to the flag was America's way of showing respect and gratitude for men and women who fought and died for America's freedoms. Active men and women in uniform of all branches of service to the United States were given due respect, always.

Although respect for the flag was exhibited at various times and for various occasions, we knew all of them. When the local flag flew at half-mast, someone had died and was deserving of America's ceremonial attention and respect.

When a casket brought a fallen American hero home from the war, it was draped in the U.S. flag. As the body deplaned, everyone stood at attention along with the president of the United States and the military personnel who accompanied the body home. At the grave site, the United States flag was ceremonially folded, saluted, and given to the widow or parent of our fallen heroes.

Everyone saluted the flag by standing at attention—left arm at their side and right hand over their heart. Gentlemen wearing hats removed them with their right hand, placed them over their hearts, and joined in the verbal Pledge of Allegiance. This was respect at its finest and every American child learned it that way.

Today, students can opt out of paying respect for anything. They call adults by their first names. Many do not respond to direction or correction. It is not necessarily considered disrespectful to curse or use profanity to authority figures.

In many schools, children can decide not to pay respect to the flag. They can sit, sleep, or even chat during the Pledge of Allegiance. They can and some do cite religious beliefs as reasons not to pay respect. Other schools offer a moment of silence and others offer no legitimate respect.

No matter where we were, unless we were crippled, dumb, blind, and could not stand, we sprang to our feet and placed our hands over our hearts when we heard the Star-Spangled Banner.

Whatever the noise level before a teacher entered the room, anyone could hear a pin drop when they entered. The next noise anyone heard was the collective voices of that classroom greeting "Good morning, teacher."

We did not learn this respect by osmosis. We were taught what to be grateful for, what to respect, and how to give reverence and honor to others. As we grew we learned *why* it was important.

Sarah taught me that there was something bigger than me that I was bound to respect. Our children have a hole in their souls when they are not taught respect for self and others. What has happened that America has this societal cancer growing in it? How do we mend this hole in our soul?

Chapter Nine

Responsibility the Hard Way

THE HOUSE WAS a lonely place as I slowly recovered from a damaged nervous system and paralysis caused by polio. As my grandmother carried me from place to place, I had spent two years of my life learning to walk again. Those were the longest two years of this growing boy's life.

From the large front picture window I leaned against, I was frustrated watching the other boys my age go and come from school. They rode bicycles, arm wrestled, threw footballs across my lawn, and played leap frog. I wanted to play too—kickball, softball, any ball—I just wanted to play. I wanted my turn at that bat! When I was able to attend school, I was already behind my friends socially. It was next to impossible to gain their respect.

I had been asking my grandmother for a pet for a long time. I wanted to play with something. She was thinking about it. I knew when she was thinking hard about something because she looked puzzled.

One day she told me that a family friend had a goat, and I could have him provided I went up town and walked him back home. There was never an agreement with Sarah without some element of responsibility attached to it.

I had visited this family friend for a few years, and they used to visit Sarah when she was too busy with me to go out much. I knew where they lived but I wasn't too sure of how to get there. "How would I get that goat home?" I thought. If I wanted that goat I had better figure that out and fast before Sarah changed her mind about the entire thing.

The next morning I started out. The further I got away from home, the more I questioned how badly I really wanted that goat. When I no longer recognized familiar neighborhood sights I knew there was no turning back so I kept going.

The Long Ride to Town

The early morning bus uptown was filled with people rushing to work. Sitting on that bus I watched the neighborhoods change colors from all black passengers, to black and white passengers, and finally to all white passengers.

People were very friendly. Some chatted about the weather. Some read the daily news. Others eavesdropped on conversations of people sitting next to them.

I was a boy of eight years riding this big green and white trolley bus. People stared at me with investigative concerns. It must have been obvious that I was very afraid. I watched with wonder through the high windows as the beautiful city unveiled itself to me street by street.

On visits to these friends, I had played with the goat but how would he be as my own pet? I wondered whether the goat would come with me willingly. If not, how was I going to get him back to Can Park?

I mused myself in thought. He was not a cat so he couldn't sit on my lap but I could pet him all day. He was not a dog. He could not fetch the newspaper. I would still have to go get it. I would have to pay a lot of attention to everything he did because if he ever got on Sarah's nerves, I could be in real trouble. I have to admit that would be funny though. And since he would be living outside, I would have lots of space for us to run around and play.

In the midst of tall men in suits and smiling women in colorful summer print dresses I stepped off of the bus. I passed large insurance companies, libraries, and museums and finally arrived at the big white house. I picked Billy up and thanked the lady. "Go straight home," she admonished in a firm, compassionate voice. I tied the rope around the goat's neck and waited to see what he was going to do. He looked at me as if he was ready to go. I looked down the long street, tugged the rope, and the goat followed me without a problem. We started the long walk back to Can Park.

The humidity and heat of the Savannah day was already evident. The sky was cloudy and it was supposed to rain. The sidewalk was so hot I felt my sandals sticking to the pavement. People interrupted their conversations and smiled at me. Couples stood along the sidewalk drinking tall glasses of cool lemonade and fanning themselves with their hats.

Backyard swimming pools were filled with children enjoying a morning swim. It rained on and off. I rested under store overhangs and in doorways. Although Sarah had often warned me not to stand under trees when it rained, trees were often the only shelter on our path.

Women were concerned about me. They offered me water and soft drinks, but it would be sudden death if my grandmother ever found out I accepted something from a stranger so I politely declined and kept walking.

As evening drew we neared Can Park. I was hungry and very thirsty. My throat was as dry as the cotton in Mr. Charlie's field. My head throbbed and I was dizzy. The goat was thirsty too. He stopped frequently and lapped from small ponds of rain water.

When we arrived home, I was exhausted. I showed Billy to my grandmother and tied him to the front tree stoop that Sarah and I had prepared for him. Sarah sent me to take a bath telling me I smell like all outdoors.

She came to my bedroom with a bowl of neck bones and white potatoes soup. I was sound asleep lying on the bed with one leg in my pajamas and the other one hanging off the side of my bed. She quietly put the lights out, backed out of the room, and closed the door.

The next day she asked me what I had planned to name him explaining that if I gave the pet a name, he would come to me when I called him. I liked that. I named him Billy.

We had so much fun. I was the alpha, and I liked being in control. Billy was not always happy with that, but at all times, he loved me unconditionally.

Unconditional Love

Finally, I had a friend that would love me unconditionally and not judge me either because I was behind my peers or that I limped when I walked because of the polio. This friend cared about me and I loved him. We came to depend on each other. I could depend on him meeting me every day after school. We walked through bushy areas so he could graze in the greener pastures. We walked because he ate, drank a lot of water, and voided every three or four hours.

Billy was a flat-footed goat and was able to steady himself on steady terrain. He even supported me during hiking and backpacking in the woods behind the house. He became my hiking buddy. Every day after homework and my other chores were complete Sarah made me drag bales of hay and alfalfa for him to eat. Billy supported many of them on his back. If I had to get them for him he had to help carry them.

This was a big responsibility, and when I did not want to do it, Sarah reminded me, not always gently, that it had been my choice to get the pet, and my choices carried responsibilities.

Most of the time, I was able to get Billy to a place where he could void, but sometimes he relieved himself wherever he happened to be standing. It was a job to clean it up. I dare not complain; after all, I wanted the pet, right?

I was always looking for some place to tie him up outside. I tied him to the back gate. He chewed himself loose and chased a chicken through the neighborhood. Of course, I had to catch him and bring him back. One time he climbed our neighbors' tree. That tree was the highest tree in Can Park. I had to go up and bring him down. He was curious about everything including my homework, Sarah's jewelry, and clothing from the clotheslines. I was always in trouble over that goat.

No matter what I was doing when Billy needed something, Sarah called me to fix the problem. She was very clear about the responsibility for this pet and she never let me forget.

Goats Are Not Sheep

One day after school, I ran home excited and completely out of breath. I slammed the door behind me and ran to the back door past my grandmother who was picking string beans over the kitchen sink. I asked her where my sheep was. Sarah recognized a teaching moment when she saw it. That day, she used my pet goat to give me a full education.

"Sheep? Sheep?" She laughed a belly laugh and echoed her words over and over. "Sit down son," she said and the lesson began. From the look on her face I knew I'd be there for a while.

"Goats are not sheep and sheep are not goats," she said as she raised and lowered her voice on every word. "Male goats rear on their hind legs and they lunge downward to butt heads. Goats have short and pointy tails. Sheep have short hanging tails," she continued. "Most goats have beards. Sheep do not have beards," and on and on she went and we laughed.

Sarah did not simply force me to accept the responsibility for the pet; she always used life to teach me a lesson that would help develop my character. Because she did, I became more and more confident in myself. I learned to perceive things I thought were impossible to be achievable. I was able to challenge my health setbacks and understand how to remove barriers in my life that hindered me.

In Sarah's house, I was not allowed to use the words "can't" or "sorry." She said those words shattered my self-esteem and self-confidence and they would keep me from being all I could be. Negative words were not allowed.

One day after school, Billy and I were playing in the yard and he head butted me. Sarah was standing a short distance away. Although she never said anything to me, the look on her face said she did not like what had happened. The next morning, I awoke early for school and ran to the back yard to see Billy. He was gone and I never saw him again. I missed him terribly and promised myself that when I was old enough, I would get another pet but a dog this time, maybe a Doberman pinscher. I was hooked and I didn't mind the responsibility that would come with it.

As an adult man, I got into dog training. I went from behavior and obedience training to activity training. Over the next few years I learned show grooming, handling, and leash training.

I fell in love with Doberman pinschers. They seemed to be the most intelligent, alert, and loyal animal to have as a friend. Careful breeding of the Doberman has improved the disposition of the breed once used as guard dogs. Males have a masculine, noble appearance. Females are usually thinner but not spindly.

HOWARD N. HUNTER

Eventually, I would train three Dobermans: Hawk, Ceasar, and Zeus. Although Hawk was my favorite, each had proud, watchful, determined, and obedient temperaments. All had titles.

Our personalities complemented each other. They were fearless. They were energetic, loyal, lively, and suitable for companionship much like Billy. I was protective of them and confident that they loved the family. They required constant attention, and I enjoyed giving it. Neither of us did well if we were separated for long periods.

I was assertive. They respected me as the alpha. It was a great relationship. Billy taught me that it was best to socialize the animals and I transferred those skills to my Dobermans. All three of the Dobermans excelled in the trainings and did well with positive reinforcements and fairness.

Working with the Dobermans taught me that the world is only a big scary place if you viewed it from a fragile point of view. I decided to use my personal challenges to help me grow and expand my world. Are you ready to meet your challenges head on, to take one step at a time into your positive future?

Get ready to see responsibility for what it is worth. Responsibility is your *response* to your *ability* and to *act* on something. Learn to use your ability to respond to situations at the highest level of your ability. When you do that, you will be able to stare down issues and see large boulders as mere steps to what you can achieve. Make the best of your future. Start today. Self-confidence is an acquired ability and in some ways the most important you will need to develop.

No one can be self-confident for you, but you. Self-confidence puts success within your reach. Accept no one's limitations placed upon you. When you know yourself, you will know your possibilities and your limitations. Think out of the box. Set your affections high. Shoot for the moon and even if you land among the stars you will still be successful.

Chapter Ten

What's Love Got to Do with Anything?

MY GRANDMOTHER WAS the first woman who quintessentially loved me. Few, if any of my relationships have ever been as intense as her love for me. Her love stabilized me. My memories of her still discipline me. I based my associations and sought happiness on that pleasant first love experience looking for her female qualities in every woman I met.

Sarah understood me. She understood that I was a black male growing up in a society where the deck was stacked against me. She told me that the greatest challenge I would face in love was taking the responsibility of it. She inspired me to settle for nothing less than the beauty love represents and compelled me to let nothing destroy my spirit, drive, or integrity in pursuit of that love.

My Whole World Ended the Moment She Left Me

My grandmother and I had lived in Connecticut for fourteen long months. The move up north was less than exciting, certainly not what either of us expected. The stress was taking a toll on her. She always appeared to be depressed or very angry.

We lived in a poor and violent community called "The Bottom" off of Windsor Street in Hartford, Connecticut, but I was tough enough for it. The hidden agenda of the street was to prove I was not girlish. Boys competed against each other in sports and playing the dozens.

We had to avoid everything feminine, yet show tenderness, and had to be strong and smart while being "cool." Each had better win or they had better be able to pay the street price.

One day I was running home from school, Sarah watched me from the window of our two-story tenement, and our eyes met. "Where do you think you are going, son?" She spoke softly. "Home," I gasped out of breath and broke into a slow saunter. "You don't have a home as long as that boy is chasing you." she continued.

She was stern and unsympathetic of the fact that the boy was twice my size. Sarah allowed no excuses. I had to prove to her that I was not running away from any situation. I realized that I had to fight someone that day, either that boy who was chasing me or my grandmother. I chose that neighborhood boy. Just knowing my grandmother was watching for the win, I beat that boy to a pulp. Then I got to go home.

Pool Hall Thugs

I fought my way past the pool hall every day. The men in that pool hall were callous and uncaring. They challenged me to become a loser as they were. They teased me for going to school, laughed at my uniform, threatened to throw my books away, took my lunch money, and offered me grown women who were willing to do all sorts of vile and inhuman things to me.

They were high school dropouts, drunks, potheads, and dead beat dads. Some had never been inside of a schoolroom. Those who were not running from the law were effectively running out of time. They cared nothing about the fact that they lacked the tools to be fruitful or productive in society, and they cared less about anything else.

With few positive role models I consistently measured myself against the low street standards paraded before me. Watching those guys often in fear of my life forced me to come to grips with society's image of black men as worthless societal parasites.

I was adjusting to a new school, neighborhood, friends, and family and we had successfully made it through the challenge of the early winter holidays. Then Sarah was in the hospital.

On February 14, I arrived home from school with a Valentine's Day card and had planned to take it to my grandmother in the hospital. I was told by a relative not to bother to go to the hospital; in fact, my grandmother had died that morning. I asked if I could see her in the hospital and they said children were not allowed in the hospital.

Standing in the doorway of the living room, my legs felt like rubber under me. I was paralyzed and for a moment I forgot to breathe. I was helpless and filled with despair. Complete shock. I was blinded by the tears leaping from my eyes as I played the news over and over in my head.

I stood still. My body felt hot, then cold. I closed my eyes because something new was stirring inside of me. Then I felt, rather than heard, a soft voice say, "Son, I will never leave you. Honor me by keeping my teachings in your heart. My words will always keep you. I will always love you. I will always be with you." Sarah's voice was whisper soft.

Sarah had taught me that I could overcome anything but she never prepared me for her eventual death. I looked around at the strangers in my life. Some tried to comfort me. They told me she was old, had lived a long life, and that she loved me dearly. Others said she was in a better place. I was hearing none of it. I wanted her back. I wanted to at least say goodbye.

My life became moment to moment and every moment seemed bleaker than the one before. I was unsure of the world and everything in it. My grandmother had been my world and her love for me represented everything in my world. It was quite obvious that no one wanted to inherit a teenage boy that they hardly knew. What was I going to do now?

My grandmother taught me compassion, empathy, and gratitude. She told me to take love everywhere and no matter what, to persevere over adversity. Her love taught me how to love God, family, and eventually to love life.

It has been more than sixty years since her death and it seems like yesterday. I cry today when I think about her as I did that many years ago. I love her for being there for me when I was lost and needed someone to love me. She is my *She-Ro*.

Chapter Eleven

Up Against the Wall

AFTER SARAH DIED I bounced back and forth between my new family members, a few months here and a few months there. At fourteen years old, I was forced to rent and share a community room. I had a job working in the ice plant at night for eleven dollars a week. I paid seven dollars a week for the room and board. I went to school in the daytime.

I shared the room with an older West Indian gentleman. That man did not even know I existed. He didn't talk to me or acknowledge me in any way. I slept on one side of the room and he slept on the other.

Sarah had taught me that one day I would be a man, but I did not think it would come so soon. In the fourteen months after her death I lost my family, dropped out of school, and was homeless.

She said work hard, love your elders, get good grades, and let God take care of the rest. While this was encouraging, her voice grew softer and softer as life got harder and harder. Today, her words are clearer than ever and they mean more to me than ever before.

The servicemen had begun returning from the war. Jobs were scarce and literally nonexistent especially for young black men who also happened to be high school dropouts.

In the defensive position of having all educational, housing, and employment opportunities exhausted, my back was truly against the wall. My survivor mentality was taking a beating.

When my back is against the wall, I tend to make quick, calculated, and conscious decisions to change my defensive posture to an offensive one. I had one hope, the United States military. I anchored my thoughts in that hope and held on because it was a difficult hope at best.

The military provided a great opportunity through the government tuition assistance programs, the Montgomery GI Bill and the Marine

Corps College Fund. It was a great alternative to living on the streets. I could commit to my country, travel the world, wear that sharp uniform, get a college education, and ultimately become one of the best the military would have to offer. How hard could that be?

I would have to pass a physical which included an eye test and chart. Reading was not the problem, seeing was. Seeing the chart would be difficult since a childhood accident had left me blind in my right eye.

My buddy and I enlisted in the U.S. Navy. He passed his physical and other tests and shipped out. I failed the eye exam and was denied entry into the navy. No problem. That only meant I had to find a way to pass that eye exam.

My buddy knew the sad reality of my life. He asked his family to take me into their house since he was no longer there. His family agreed. I paid four dollars for the bus to get me to their apartment. I was doing excellent in school and making good grades, but eleven dollars a week was not enough money to take care of myself. The military once again became an option. I had to pass that test and get in That was all it was to it.

Over the next year, I paid three hundred and twenty visits to the Hartford recruiting office. I became a daily thorn in the recruiter's backside questioning him about naval and officer positions. The Equal Opportunity Bill for all servicemen had recently become a law so they let me come as often as I wanted and were sure to cover any signs of discrimination.

The recruiter's impressive build and authoritative appearance including great height and strong spirit intimated me. But I was determined to not let him see me sweat. He explained the rigors of basic training, drill sergeant training, classroom and physical requirements. He emphasized that only a tiny percent of people who graduate meets the expectations of the Marine Corps training and absolutely no blacks had ever qualified. He skipped pages in the brochure and rushed through the part about the role of women recruits, military haircuts and military jobs and liberty, overseas, pay rates and college as if he never expected me to need that information. I was overwhelmed but impressed.

Each time I entered that office, my eyes scanned that eye chart memorizing specific placement of every letter and number on every

HOWARD N. HUNTER

line. Every night I was motivated by the fact that I had no alternative to survival but to memorize that entire eye chart. I had to get my back up off of life's wall. The marines were going to help me do that.

The next year I enlisted at the Springfield Massachusetts Marine recruiting office and passed the physical with flying colors. The commander looked at me with concern. "Young man," he asked as he scribbled the word "PASSED" in red on my medical chart, "why the marines? Not the navy? You are so small." Before he could finish his statement, I snapped at him. "I may not be big enough but I am bad enough and I am willing to fight!" The commander flashed a side military grin, looked at the assistant, and snapped, "Sign him up. That is exactly what the marines are looking for in a recruit!" I had passed another life's test and was on my way to the United States Marine Corps.

September 20, 1949, we boarded the train at 5:00 a.m. after breakfast leaving Hartford, Connecticut, for Parris Island. I did not know it yet but I was about to experience my first military racial injustice.

White recruits boarded at the front of the train. The conductor instructed John and I to board at the rear. John was another black recruit from the Hartford area. We looked at each other and reluctantly moved to the rear.

During lunch, the white recruits came to the back of the train to get me and John. The conductor would have the last word. "Move to the front or go to jail at the next stop," he demanded. The stare in his eyes meant business and for a moment I was that little boy back in Savannah looking in the eyes of the white Ku Klux Klan. His face was red as the apples in Grandma's apple orchard. The bulging veins in his neck stood at attention assuring us he meant every word.

When we arrived at the train depot in Parris Island, South Carolina we met Sergeant Shaw, a big burly black marine. He looked directly at us. His words were few and he did not stumble. He pointed at me and John and snapped, "You and you, come with me." John and I moved quickly to his side. He directed us to a bus that would take us to Parris Island to boot camp.

On the bus, white recruits screamed hateful racial slurs at us. They promised to hang us niggers before boot camp was over. That was a long bus trip. I was reminded of a saying back in Savannah: "If a white man could not hang a black man, he would hang his black

Cadillac!" John and I were frightened. Speaking to each other through hand gestures and silent eye contacts we agreed to stick together no matter what happened. So far, not much was different than civilian life. Unfortunately, we had already grown used to this treatment. It had prepared us to shoulder the weight of this type of racism. There was nowhere to run or hide and certainly no turning back. Eyes to the sky and whispering a prayer I settled in and prepared for this trip down racism court.

A fine stream of colored marine recruitment posters had encouraged us to be the first to fight. Colorful brochures portrayed sunny beaches with silver sands under bright, bold sunshines. Our mouths watered over the possibility of fine travel in far away lands with beautiful, smiling women warmly welcoming us.

The posters showed us erect standing marines in sharp blue and red uniforms, which we came to know as our Dress Blues, compelling us to join them to be the first to fight. They were sharp. Every man standing in line with the crease down the center of his pants leg, white uniform shirt and black shoes shinning like brand new pennies I wanted to look like that.

They promised tuition-free college education and life-long, world wide opportunities and careers. But nothing I ever read prepared me for what I was experiencing on this cold, dark, and scary night or for anything I would eventually face living in Uncle Sam's house.

We were angry and disheartened. We had signed on the dotted line agreeing to fight to our death to protect the freedoms of the United States and we, ourselves, were not free.

African-Americans and whites were segregated from each other and the rigor of the Marine Corps recruit showed no discrimination. No matter the color of your skin you had better be unflinching. Everyone had to exceed the strenuous requirements and conquer the rigid challenges. Without a doubt if marine boot camp couldn't make you a man, no one or nothing could.

There would be no doubt about why we were on that island. We were going to become marines! We were going to become men. First, we were going to face the physical and mental preparation called basic training, next rifle training, and finally field training. And in case we were unsure, we were informed that we were in the best outfit in the world and we were there for only one purpose: to be made into marines.

HOWARD N. HUNTER

Anyone who was not physically ready upon reaching that island would be ready when they left it. The marines had a solution for that called the Physical Conditioning Platoon. Time was a dutiful element. We ate, slept, ran, and performed sit-ups and pull-ups from time to time. We marched against time and at all times we respected time. No one was getting off of the island until and unless we were ready.

We received our gear and a battery of physical examinations: a strength test, weapons handling, and a master obstacle course. No doubt, this was the most difficult thing I would ever face. For one moment I questioned my grandmother's teachings to be fearless in the face of fear. Sergeant said we were there to be made into marines and it was going to be no other way.

I quickly discovered that marine boot camp was the greatest physical and mental challenge of any of Uncle Sam's military branches of service. In addition to the higher requirements, we had to adhere to the core marine values of honor, courage, and commitment while going through boot camp hell.

There would be no gifts from back home, not that I expected anything. There was mail protocol. Letters had to be addressed in your name only. Titles and ranks like "private" or "marine" had to be earned and we were busy earning them for we would earn the title of marine and that would not happen until after the Crucible.

The Crucible is the fifty-four-hour culmination to the transformation of training we had to undertake. Each level was more challenging. Conquering the Crucible involved food and sleep deprivation and the completion of various obstacles. If you did not pass them, you were never going to be a marine.

We walked for miles, conquering several problem-solving exercises at thirty-six different stations with only three "ready-to-eat" meals within the fifty hours.

We carried ammunition cans of up to fifty pounds and dummies weighing up to one hundred pounds in addition to our gear, uniform, and service rifles. The Crucible was the test that separated the boys from the men, the girls from the women, and all marines from other branches of service.

Every hardship in my life had prepared me for this and I was going to prove I was ready. Military life was the path to success that

I had chosen but believe me I was having no picnic. If I was going to succeed at it, I had better make it happen. Parris Island, here I come.

Parris Island

Parris Island is the place where marines are made. It always has been and it will always be the place where marines are made. You come to Parris Island with what you have but you leave Parris Island a marine. There is no doubt about that.

We arrived on the island at midnight in the middle of blanket darkness. Its area was blacker than one hundred midnights in a Georgia swamp. The moon reflected the shark-infested waters. Silhouettes of large fins reflected off of the shine of the moon.

We could see nothing, but we could hear sharks sharpening their teeth. The eerie silence sent my imagination into overdrive and there was no turning back. The white sergeant cold-stared through the souls of every man on that bus. I'd hoped he could not read my thoughts.

Standing at the front of the bus with his rifle positioned, he offered us three choices of getting off of that island. He said we could swim the shark-infested waters, we could leave with the flag at half-mast, or we could graduate as proud marines. I made an immediate decision and chose to do what it takes to become a marine.

When we arrived at the second battalion, the sergeant commanded a white marine to take me and John to our barracks. The other white marines remained on the bus. I wondered where they were going.

Surprise! Surprise! The barracks housed all black marines. All black marines from the east coast were commanded to eat together and consequences were to be had if those restrictions were not adhered to. We were together under the banner of the United States Marines but not much was different. We could not help each other and we whispered in disgust about our poor living conditions.

Before day, Sergeant Shaw entered our barracks with a harkening voice like a bullhorn echo. "Able! Hockaday! Hunter! Susberry! Fall out!" He escorted us to Sergeant Kelly and Sergeant Wyconski who took us to the First Battalion, Platoon 81 for further training.

We were the first four black men separated from the group who would eventually become Pariss Island graduates. We were chosen to integrate Platoon 81. Platoon 80 had been integrated before Platoon 81 but Platoon 81 was the first integrated platoon to graduate. Platoon 80 graduated the day after Platoon 81.

The barracks held about twenty-five black men and none of us knew each other. We were all pissed off about the unfair treatment and frightened to let anyone know what we were thinking.

We used silent communications we had learned back at home, reading lips, interpreting looks, deciphering facial expressions and head nods and talking with our eyes as we passed each other in the halls. It was a form of communication learned during early slavery and passed from generation to generation and family to family. That unspoken language came in handy. Complete conversations were held through hand motions, stares, and glances. On Sunday, we went to the chapel and took advantage of the opportunity to speak to each other.

Most blacks knew the silent language. We had been raised with parents and grandparents who never needed to speak a word to be understood. They just looked at us and the message was clear.

The four black pioneers, Able, Hockaday, Hunter, and Susberry were assigned to Platoon 81. They had many fights with the eighty-four marines in the platoon. The grandson of John Wilkes Booth was in that same platoon. We got along like oil and water. He loved to use that disgusting word "nigger" and I hated it. His tongue would get stuck on it. I think he used to say it in his sleep. He certainly sang it in the shower and he would say it whenever he saw me.

One day he told me, "You niggers are not good enough to be marines." I tried to rip his tongue out of his mouth and his skin off of his back. I was already angry at the conditions and the treatment we received and was in no mood to be further disrespected.

Booth thought he was special because his grandfather had made a name for himself by murdering President Abraham Lincoln. That did not hold water with me. He was just another murderer. Sergeant Kelly witnessed the fight and halted it when he saw me land a few good blows to Booth's head.

Able, Hockaday, Susberry, and I had become brothers and best friends. They vowed that if the disrespect continued they would be next to get a sweet taste of Wilkes Booth. If that meant kicking ass and taking names we were ready. We had taken nonsense on the street and left it there; signed the dotted line to sacrifice our lives in Uncle Sam's service and shed our blood around the world to become proud marines. No one was going to stop us.

We kept our eyes on each other at all times. While two of us slept, two stood watch. We slept with our bayonets ready to kill whomever failed to step to us right. We lived like that and became closer than brothers.

Indeed one of us had a fight every day until Sergeant Kelly decided to make the two fighting men give each other bear hugs. We worked hard to avoid fights once he started that. The last thing we wanted to do was to hug some guy we were fighting.

Fixing each of us in his gaze, Sergeant Kelly released a rebuke that neither of us would forget. "Men, you are marines!" he chided. "Every marine is your brother! Every marine is important! Once a marine, always a marine! When one marine is attacked, all marines are attacked!" And then he said something that fused our fates forever. "You had better be willing to live together because you are certainly going to die together!" Besides not wanting to give another man a hug, every other marine was all any marine had. If we planned to go home, we had better recognize that fact and begin to act civilized.

There was a challenge between drill instructors to graduate an honor platoon and pass top-notch inspections. In order to be an honor platoon, we had to respect and help each other all the way to ensure all of us graduated. If not, we were all going to suffer the consequences.

The fighting and disrespect stopped. Brotherhood, respect, and unity became the new platoon goal. After twelve weeks of training, drilling, inspection, and parading, we graduated an honor platoon with Able as the honor flag bearer! We were finally marine brothers.

Some of us forgot the rest of the world had not experienced what we had endured and learned to love and support each other.

A few of the white marine brothers invited me to come home with them to Alabama and Mississippi and other places in the south. They had a point to make with family and friends back home. They wanted to prove to them that black people were okay and that what they had believed for hundreds of years was not true.

Black people didn't have a tail like a monkey. The color of their skin did not rub off. It did not wash off in the shower, nor were they sooty people like our families had taught us. They had real families just like white people, too. They wanted their families to see me eat so they could prove to them that black people taught their children table manners just like whites. My white marine brothers may have been naïve, but I was smarter than that.

I had traveled across the world and was still safe. I was not going to get lynched so they could prove their point to anyone. What would I look like going into the deep king cotton picking south of popular hostility where people lacked sound knowledge to allow someone to prove a point about who I was? This marine brother may have had an epiphany but I doubted if his family had one.

Many southerners had never seen black people other than in cartoons or as servants. Their perceptions of black men were derived entirely from assertions or personal values. I was not the sacrificial lamb to prove them wrong. I relied upon something I learned in one of Sarah's Sunday evening dinner chats. Self-preservation is the first law of Mother Nature and I thought this was a good time to apply this good sanity.

I refused those invitations. We graduated as brothers and friends on December 13, 1949. I never saw the white brothers again and often wondered if they ever proved their point to their southern families.

I was assigned to Camp Lejeune, North Carolina for advance training and general orders for all new marines. I had made it. I had come a long way from sneaking around enlistment offices and memorizing eye charts. Finally, I was one of the few, one of the proud. I had become a proud United States Marine.

Although there were two integrated platoons—Platoon 80 and Platoon 81. Platoon 81 was the first integrated, graduated platoon. That was my platoon. Here are pictures of both platoons. The few blacks in these platoons were truly proud because we had become United States Marines.

Platoon 80

HOWARD N. HUNTER

Platoon 81

Howard N. Hunter pointing at himself at the Parris Island Museum.

Camp Lejeune

Arriving at Camp Lejeune was exciting and a happy rest from the stringent rules of boot camp. Barns, farmhouses, and tents welcomed us. The remote pine forest and miles of beaches made Camp Lejeune an ideal training base. The weather was perfect and many units had been deployed there.

On May 1, 1941, Lieutenant Colonel William P. T. Bill was ordered by the seventeenth commandant lieutenant general, then mayor general, Thomas Holcomb, to establish and assume command of the base known as Marine Barracks New River, North Carolina. His original headquarters was located at Montford Point where black marines were trained separate from white marines. In August of 1942, it was moved to building #1 at Hadnot Point where it remains today.

Near the end of 1942, the base took on the name of Camp Lejeune, named in honor of the thirteenth commandant and commanding general of the Second Army Division in World War I, Major General John A. Lejeune. After the walls of segregation came down, a part of the base was named in honor of Sergeant Major Johnson. Marine Corps Service support schools were located there.

Though the walls of racism had begun to tumble, racism was still very obvious. Fellow black marines were much older but less tanked than white marines in barracks that housed both blacks and whites. The barracks sat at a right angle with whites on one side, blacks on the other. We worked separate details classified as white and black details.

Rules for passing inspection were discriminatory. General inspections were held at the same time. The standard was set by the white marine brothers. White marines were inspected in the front of the barracks and black marines were inspected at the rear.

If white marines passed inspection, everyone was automatically granted liberty. If white marines failed general inspections, black marines automatically failed and no one went on liberty. The entire platoon paid the price when the white marine brothers failed inspection. If black marines failed inspection, white marines were still granted liberty. Black marines were assigned to drill and practice. No liberty for us.

No Black Officers Now—You will Not Be the First!

I entered the marines with a burning desire to become an officer. I had proven that I was ready and I had what it took to become a marine. I trained hard, overcame physical barriers, and developed the leadership skills to become an officer. I wanted the respect of my peers, the loyalty of my fellow marines and I could taste the gratitude of Americas as I led the United States Marine to victory under my command.

I learned about marine life from the older black marines. I was young with a big mouth and bigger ideas. I believed what Sarah told me: work hard, trust God, and I could achieve anything. It was obvious to them that I was still wet behind the ears. The brothers took me under their wings and many times they bailed me out of trouble. I developed into manhood under their male nurturing.

One time Sergeant finished his commands and hypothetically asked the men if they had any questions. Every man in the barracks sat silently still except me. I raised my hand. My brother, next to me, dropped his shaking head toward the floor and sighed, "Sarg," I went on, "I want to know why I can't have seconds in the chow hall."

Sergeant focused me in his gaze, "*Seconds*! *Seconds*!" he bellowed. His eyes widened further. "Gunny! You want seconds?" He shouted. "Yes, sir, I don't get enough to eat." I continued. I felt all eyes on my back. I turned my head slowly to the brother on the right. His face was white as snow. "You want seconds?" Sergeant screamed again. "Two weeks mess hall duty! Dizzzed-mizzzed!"

I was a young gunny with a big mouth. My brothers never let me forget that. A few weeks with the older black marines and I had not learned to keep my mouth shut. I had many such experiences before I learned when to talk and when to shut up.

Another time Captain Eastman asked me what I wanted to do during my enlistment. With a proud marine stature I saluted and announced proudly, "I want to become a marine officer, Sir!" The collective gasp from my big brothers sucked the oxygen out of the room. The white officer stepped so close to me our eyes melded. I could feel the heat of his breath as he scouled at me, "Son, we have no black officers in these United States Marines and you will not be

HOWARD N. HUNTER

the first! Do you understand me, Private?" "Yes, Sir," I retorted. With that exchange, my military dream became a nightmare.

My enlistment orders reflected that I played the trumpet in my high School band. The white officer quipped, "The Marine Corps Band?" Stomping my dream to become an officer and with that fire in my belly I joined the Marine Corps Band. Another dream deferred as I was off to music school.

I remember thinking this is the U.S. Marines. This could not be racism that broke individual spirits and made people weak. The marines were the strongest branch of service and prided themselves on making boys into marines. Sure felt like getting kicked out of white restaurants and being forbidden to drink from white water fountains to me. Felt like pure racism to me.

Chapter Twelve

Mine Eyes Have Seen the Glory
The Montford Point Marines!

THE YEAR 2008 was a historically defining year for our nation. My eyes have seen the glory of the leveling of the playing field. I witnessed the glorious nomination of a black man named Barack Obama for the president of the United States of America.

On January 2009, Barack Obama became the first black president of the United States. Barack and I share a similar genetic code being of mixed black and white heritage. Like Barack, I championed causes for the betterment of this society. As the first black president of the United States, Barack is a trailblazer. As one of the first four black men to integrate the U.S. Marines, so was I. His work will speak for him. Mine will speak for me.

I read the following article in the *Hartford Courant* newspaper discussing the rarity of black officers in the United States military services. We have come a long way, but we are not home yet.

The pressure being applied to Barack Obama as U.S. president was expected. He's been a black man long enough to know that he'd be held to a standard higher than any other U.S. president.

He expected this country to hold him responsible for everything that had gone wrong in the United States since George Washington was president! He knew there would be those who expected him to solve all problems for every group and for everyone.

He probably also wanted to believe that the color lines in this country had been neutralized. He believed what we all wanted to believe that America was ready for the best of change for all of her people. Unfortunately, we still have a long way to go.

How long will it take for this nation to truly strive for equality for her people? As black people, we have always been expected to do more with less under undue pressure.

I had hoped with our president for the best cooperation but he would never get it. One thing is for sure, he will leave the presidency destroying an old myth that blacks are not qualified or smart enough to be in leadership. No one can take that away from him.

If I called the name of Colin Powell, most people would know him from his duties as the chairman of the Joint Chiefs of Staff under President George Herbert Walker Bush or his role in the Desert Storm. But before Colin Powell was born in Harlem in 1937, black men were already fighting for the United States.

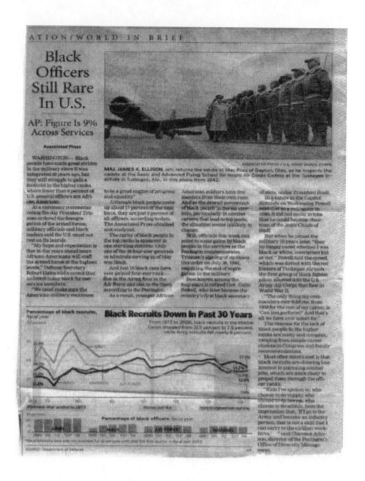

Ref: The Hartford Courant, Thursday, July 12, 2008 Page A2

Hartford Courant Article

From 1775 until after President Roosevelt signed an executive order in June 1941 establishing fair employment practices in the armed forces, blacks were prohibited from serving in the United States Marine Corps.

Although blacks had a positive performance record serving the army and navy since recorded history, the presidential directive was not well received by the Marine Corps commandant, who at the time stated, "There would be a definite loss of efficiency in the Marine Corps if we have to take Negroes." African-Americans were allowed to enlist in the Marine Corps in 1942.

HOWARD N. HUNTER

In compliance, the Marine Corps, with $750,000 dollars constructed a recruit training facility for the sole purpose of administering basic training to African-American recruits.

The facility was located on the Lejeune Marine Corps Base at New River, North Carolina. And although they were separated from the main camp of white recruits by twelve miles of dense forest, very few people knew of its existence; twenty thousand blacks were trained there and had integrated the U.S. Marines. It was called Montford Point Camp.

The men of Montford Point were mistreated, and not allowed to go to neighboring all-white camps without being accompanied by a white marine. They were often arrested for nonsense such as "impersonating" a marine because they were wearing a marine uniform.

In 1949, President Truman signed an executive order to force full integration of the United States Marines. The footprints of the Montford Point Marines were left on the beaches of Saipan, Guam, Peleliu, Iwo Jima, and Okinawa.

The first commanding officer of Montford Point was Colonel Samuel A. Woods. He fought against discrimination and for fairness for black marines. He became known as the "White Father."

By May 1943, an adequate number of African-American sergeants and corporals had been trained to replace all White Drill instructors; and an African-American sergeant, "Hashmark" Johnson, bore the title of 61 Recruit Battalion Field Sergeant Major.

In 1965, a reunion of marines was held in Philadelphia, Pennsylvania. More than four hundred former and active Montford Point marines from all over the country attended and established the Montford Point Marines Association to preserve proper military history.

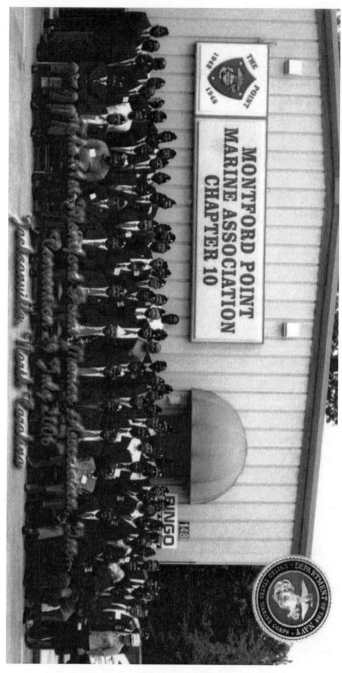

The Forty-first Montford Point
Marines Association Inc. 29th Convention,
2006, Chapter 10, Jacksonville, North Carolina

HOWARD N. HUNTER

Though these men served valiantly, they were not allowed to graduate. The first integrated black platoon was Platoon 80. The first integrated platoon to graduate was Platoon 81. I am proud to have been a member of that historic class.

The captain who screamed at me that the marines had no black officers and I would not be the first was right—I was not the first. But I have been blessed to live long enough to witness the first and many other black officers and generals in the United States Marine Corps. For a trailblazer like myself that has to be good enough.

Black Generals at Montford Point
Convention with Commandant

General Gaskins with Montford Point Veterans

As you see from the pictures, none of these Generals are new recruits. They are all seasoned members of the Montford Point marines who are part of the gently woven fabric of America.

They fought to protect this nation when this nation offered them no basic civil rights. I respect these heroes for their courageous acts. They proved that they were the very best by challenging a system that dared them to be men.

Weighted down with prejudice they towed the line, stared down bigotry and endemic racial disparages that separated black men from white men.

It is disheartening to know that their grandchildren and great-grandchildren have never heard a positive story about these great courageous men who gave their lives and service with great integrity for this country.

I want to make an honorable mention here about a man who has stuck closer to me than a brother. Many people know the Honorable Walter "Doc" Hurley and for those of you who have not had the

HOWARD N. HUNTER

pleasure, you have missed an extraordinary opportunity in your lives.

I met Doc Hurley in 1948 at an all-star basketball game in Springfield, Massachusetts. I was attending Hartford High School. Doc Hurley had completed his military career in the United States Marines.

I met him at the game and he recognized me. We have been friends ever since. He became my mentor. I began modeling him for he was a man of distinction and I wanted to be just like him. I followed him to different sports games where he was a referee. When I went to boot camp and returned, we renewed our friendship. At the time he introduced me to the men of Montford Point and their service because he had been one of them.

Doc is a real man. He was an educator. I became an educator. I just admire the man. He has retired now from formal education but he is still teaching. You can find him any day of the week encouraging any young person to be their best.

The Honorable Walter Doc Hurley & Mr. Howard Hunter

I want to encourage anyone reading this book who may be the grandchild or great-grandchild of any of these courageous men to seek out their memory. Seek people who will tell you positive stories of their courage, patriotism, and their lives. Read this and other books on the subject of the Montford Point Marines. You will find their lives and character to be extraordinaire.

Our success as a people could not have been achieved without the strength of mind, fortitude, and grit of the men of Montford Point. The Montford Pointers played a crucial role in bringing segregation to an end in the United States and in fighting the Second World War, the Korean Conflict, and the Vietnam War.

HOWARD N. HUNTER

If you take nothing else away from these men, try to view their struggles as an opportunity for your personal growth. In situations where you know you are right or when anyone questions your judgment, stay the course even if the world stands against you. You will prevail. They did. This nation owes a debt of gratitude to the Montford Pointers who persevered and stayed the course through the dark days of negativity.

My Montford Point marine brothers can take their rightful place in the annals of the United States Marine Corps history. I was lucky enough to meet many of them and have enclosed some pictures of different events in this writing for your enjoyment.

ROOSEVELT EXECUTIVE ORDER 8802

Reaffirming Policy Of Full Participation In The Defense Program By All Persons, Regardless Of Race, Creed, Color, Or National Origin, And Directing Certain Action In Furtherance Of Said Policy
June 25, 1941: "WHEREAS it is the policy of the United States to encourage full participation in the national defense program by all citizens of the United States, regardless of race, creed, color, or national origin, in the firm belief that the democratic way of life within the Nation can be defended successfully only with the help and support of all groups within its borders; and WHEREAS there is evidence that available and needed workers have been barred from employment in industries engaged in defense production solely because of considerations of race, creed, color, or national origin, to the detriment of workers' morale and of national unity: NOW, THEREFORE, by virtue of the authority vested in me by the Constitution and the statutes, and as a prerequisite to the successful conduct of our national defense production effort, I do hereby reaffirm the policy of the United States that there shall be no discrimination in the employment of workers in defense industries or government because of race, creed, color, or national origin, and I do hereby declare that it is the duty of employers and of labor organizations, in furtherance of said policy and of this order, to provide for the full and equitable participation of all workers in defense industries, without discrimination because of race, creed, color, or national origin; And it is hereby ordered as follows: 1. All departments and agencies of the Government of the United States concerned with vocational and training programs for defense production shall take special measures appropriate to assure that such programs are administered without discrimination because of race, creed, color, or national origin; 2. All contracting agencies of the Government of the United States shall include in all defense contracts hereafter negotiated by them a provision obligating the contractor not to discriminate against any worker because of race, creed, color, or national origin; 3. There is established in the Office of Production Management a Committee on Fair Employment Practice, which shall consist of a chairman and four other members to be appointed by the President. The Chairman and members of the Committee shall serve as such without compensation but shall be entitled to actual and

HOWARD N. HUNTER

necessary transportation, subsistence and other expenses incidental to performance of their duties. The Committee shall receive and investigate complaints of discrimination in violation of the provisions of this order and shall take appropriate steps to redress grievances which it finds to be valid. The Committee shall also recommend to the several departments and agencies of the Government of the United States and to the President all measures which may be deemed by it necessary or proper to effectuate the provisions of this order."

Franklin D. Roosevelt
The White House,
June 25, 1941

Iwo Jima

I have just a word on the subject of Iwo Jima. Keep in mind there were only two types of marines on Iwo Jima: those who were fighting and those who were waiting to fight.

There remains a burning question: were there black fighting forces on the island of Iwo Jima? History tells us that the United States captured the island from Japan on the thirty-sixth day of the fierce battle. But most deny the fact that blacks were there.

In Christopher Moore's book *Fighting for America: Black Soldiers—the Unsung Heroes of World War II,* he sets the record straight. Moore explains blacks were assigned to ammunition and supply roles and at times had to fire their rifles in battle against enemy resistance.

Don't take that statement lightly. Never was a war fought without ammunition, and certainly none has ever been won without it. If black men did not load and distribute ammunition, who was going to do it?

It is a sad reality that blacks, even when doing our part, still face discrimination. Change is slow but sure. I encourage anyone who wants to know more about this battle to research the Internet and your local research librarians will be glad to help you locate information.

Chapter Thirteen

Passing for White
America's Brown Bag Test

THE UNITED STATES had an insatiable appetite for racial injustice and they set up a specific racial "caste" system called *passing*. Passing was an ambiguous criterion qualifying people as "black" or "white." The system was to determine the amount of black blood each person had in them to allow "light" skinned people with "black" blood to pass as white people. This would insure them jobs and education that was denied darker skin people who could be identified as black.

Between 1877 and the mid-1960's Jim Crow laws represented a series of rigid anti-black laws. It was a way of life. Under Jim Crow, African-Americans were relegated to the status of second-class citizens. All major societal institutions reflected and supported the oppression of blacks.

The "one-drop" rule is a historical theory that caused a lot of confusion. The theory held that any person with any trace of African blood (even a drop) could not be considered white. In other words, if you had one drop of black blood, you were considered a black person.

Jim Crow did not make sense but it was very powerful. It was underscored by some reprehensible beliefs. It was accepted in all states that whites were superior to blacks in intelligence and had better morals.

The law held that sexual relations between blacks and whites would produce a mongrel race that would destroy the white fabric of America. They believed that treating blacks as equals would encourage interracial sexual unions and that violence should be used to keep blacks at the bottom of the racial hierarchy. Black people were categorized as followed:

- A Sacatra was a light-skinned person who was half Griffe and half black.
- A Griffe was a light-skinned person who was half black and half mulatto or an Indian.
- A Marabong was a light-skinned person who was half mulatto and half Griffe.
- A Quadroon was a light-skinned person who was half white and half mulatto.
- A Metif was a light-skinned person who was half white and half Quadroon.
- A Meamelouc was a light-skinned person who was half white and half Metif.
- A Quateron was a light-skinned person who was half white and Meamelouc.
- A Sang-mele was a light-skinned person who was half white and half Quarteron.
- A mulatto was a light-skinned person who had one-half black blood and half white blood.
- A Quadroon was a light-skinned person who had one-quarter black blood and three-quarter white blood.
- An Octoroon was the offspring of a Quadroon and a white person. This person had less than one quarter of black blood.
- A Cascos was the offspring of two mulattos and had less than one-half of black blood.
- A Sambo was the offspring of a mulatto and a black and carried less than three-quarter black blood.
- A Mango was the offspring of a Sambo and a black and carried the same amount of black blood of a Sambo.
- A Mustifee was the offspring of an Octoroon and a white and carried less than one-sixteenth of black blood.
- A Mustifino was the offspring of a Mustifee and a white and carried less than one thirty-second of black blood.

The categories where a person had less than one-quarter of black blood was the only category considered "passing" for white. The individual had to have "white" physical characteristics also.

HOWARD N. HUNTER

As people intermarried, it became more difficult to distinguish some blacks from whites. White leaders feared the consequences of the color line becoming blurred to the point of confusion. If this continued unabated they reasoned blacks would pollute the entire white race.

In 1691, laws were enacted to prevent interracial marriage between blacks and whites. By the nineteenth century, classifications of "colored" people were limited to Negroes and Mulattoes. Finally, they classified us as simply Negroes. Out of this chain of ignorance the dark skinned people were classified as blacks and today we are called African-Americans.

The military was different. Whenever I assisted a marine brother on the field or in a foxhole no one ever asked me what classification I was in and I had blue eyes!

I held onto Sarah's principles and promised to let my reputation reflect my character. I refused to take ethical shortcuts and was careful to build my character on certainty and punctuate decisions with emphases for my own good.

Chapter Fourteen

Onto Manhood

MATURING WAS GRADUAL but an honorable discharge from the marines rendered me an instant man. I no longer peeled rubber at the stoplight seeking attention nor did I have a need to wash away adolescence with a frothy six-pack. I learned to keep my potty mouth shut and exercise the privilege to make my own choices.

Fresh out of the marines, cocky and very self-aware, I designated women as my new liberty. My new battle was to win women. And I have the emotional battle scars to prove it. I went to combat for the often exchanging integrity for duplicity.

Every woman became my challenge. It became my daily task to simply balance my schedule to include them. The requirements were simple: they had to be beautiful. That was it. They simply had to look good on my arm. In exchange, I lavished them with money and gifts. Sophisticated women saw right through me but some played the game. I was no gambler and this mentality cost me more than I had to wager in relationships.

It took me a while, but I learned that a boy is a male person caught between the innocence of infancy and the dignity of manhood. All boys have the same characteristics and all boys play.

Boys refuse to take responsibility for their actions. They point fingers and blame others. They are wonderful little people that will one day become men but on their way to manhood they have much maturing to do.

Men take credit for their successes and accept responsibility for correcting their failures. You can always tell a boy from a man by the way he acts. When a boy becomes a man he stops doing "childish" things.

Boys and Women

Boys run around on women. They are boys. When I was a boy, all I wanted to do was to satisfy myself. When I became a man, I wanted to satisfy women.

As a man, I did not need multiple women to serve me, boost my ego, or act like a mother to me. I satisfied myself with good things in life and I set out to satisfy them.

As a boy, I wanted to increase the numbers in my little black book. As a man, my little black book held my weekly, monthly, and annual goals.

As a boy, I was afraid of being alone with my thoughts. As a man, I seek quiet time specifically to be alone with my thoughts.

Boys make babies. Men raise them. Boys are dependent on others and rely on others to clean up their messes. Men make few messes and clean up behind themselves. Boys make babies and go home to their mothers leaving their children and their mothers to fin for themselves.

Men are disciplined standing up for their beliefs. They have stamina, drive, and determination and have no problems admitting mistakes. They are focused, concentrated hard workers who operate from a mutual power source in relationships, not control of another.

Boys watch every female skirt as if he is unsure of its' potential. Men understand the potential and are prepared for the responsibility that comes with that female skirt. Boys disregard the value of women. Men value women and understand the charge entrusted to them for their safeguard.

Boys seek role models for direction. Men are role models providing direction. Real men do not equate emotional toughness with masculinity. On which side do you come up?

I was comfortable when I fully reached manhood. Between my grandmother and the Marine Corps, I had a firm set of values designed by loving hands of destiny and not by a street culture. I learned to ask the hard questions and accept the hard answers.

I left the marines with order in my life, determined to help create order in a chaotic world. I came out a forward logical thinker, much wiser with far greater understanding than the boy who went into the marines.

Living, Loving, Dating, and Loving It All

I had a core human need to be valued and accepted for the person I was and not for what I had to offer. But it seemed that would be the inclination of my life. I am so grateful for two women in particular for their love and patience.

Thank God for the nurturing of my grandmother. Because of her I had survived with my masculinity intact and on my own terms. I respected myself and demanded others to do the same. Because of what I learned from her, I respect women as the highest gift that God has given for the completion of men.

As a man, one of the most difficult questions I was forced to answer was "What is love?" Love does not have a one size fits all definition. Everyone must define love for themselves.

It was easier for me to define what love was not. It was more difficult defining what love is but here is my definition and it can be a starting point for you.

In many relationships where I believed myself to be in love, I disregarded myself and my own needs giving priority always to the female. I just assumed this person had my best interest at heart and stumbled into what I thought was love. I was not sure how to initiate love or stop the emotional bleeding when the relationships ended.

Many of the women whom I fell in love with will remain fresh in my heart. In many of the cases I was unprepared for the strong, emotional feelings of passion and sincerity I would experience. But my memories of them are audacious and bold, and I will always treasure them.

I celebrated with women of all races and cultures. Some were round, full, and luscious, others thin and curvy. Everyone was attractive, friendly, bright, charming, mysterious, and captivating. All made my heart throb. While they had different personalities, they each had one thing in common—they all wanted to be loved and appreciated. They each deserved a man who had come into manhood and could give them what they wanted and deserved.

When I look into my life, I wish I had taken more opportunities to date before making the serious decision to marry. I wish the adults in my life had cared enough about me to protect me from premarital intimacy as it had lasting effects on my relationships. I hope I am providing some of that parental influence to you through this book.

I had two marriages and two divorces. I entered both marriages without considering mine or the intended wife's character, beliefs, or values. Both were rocky relationships.

Divorce was not the best option but the only one since we had not given forethought, due time, and interest to the seriousness of the matter.

We vowed until death do we part; divorcing her would render me without honor and integrity. We separated, not divorced. Somehow that was not as bad as a divorce. I lived my life. She lived hers. The problem was not the divorce. It was the marriage. It should have not happened in the first place.

Many years passed and I considered that I was much more mature and I married again. Again, I married for the wrong reasons. This marriage was brief also.

It is imperative that when you decide to marry, remember to question yourself to the validity of it. Is this relationship right for you? Is this woman the right person for you? Are you the right man for this woman? Do you see eye to eye on most issues? Are the issues you do not see eye to eye on workable within the relationship? Are both people in the relationship for the same reasons and are each of you ready to work to reach amicable agreements for the betterment of the relationship?

Take the time to discuss why you each love the other. This may sound corny but marriage is not a vacation or a holiday, it should last forever. It is very hard work but taking some of the necessary steps before the marriage will help ensure a beautiful relationship beginning with the wedding ceremony. Both of you should be of good character and sound integrity.

One more thing, honesty is the best policy. No secrets right from the beginning. If these basics are not in place you are probably getting started on the wrong foot. If you think these suggestions are too stringent you'll want to check yourself and your partner again to be sure this is the right relationship for you. This will take some time but you, your partner and your relationship is worth it.

Understand this: children will come. Are you ready? Are you prepared? We live in a time when millions of black children are fatherless and motherless. They are abused, and the state-run foster care systems are overrun with "throw away" children. These children are those who were not conceived in love and moreover whose parents were not ready for the unforeseen responsibility of them.

Here are some things I learned from my personal relationships. Maybe some of them can help you as you grow.

A Word to the Boys on Sex and Sexuality

Most men believe we know how to please a woman. Many of us do not have a clue. We know how to have sex; pleasing her is entirely different. That's right I said it. Simply because you have pleasure does not mean she is pleased. We need to listen to her, not simply hear her words, but listen when she talks. What is she saying? Ask yourself everyday, what can I do today to fully appreciate this woman?

A few years ago, a very good female friend of mine laughed in my face and told me some things about women that I did not know. I had lived, traveled the world, met and associated with many women. The things she said rolled right off of her tongue to my personal embarrassment. I have told her how much I learned by talking to her. I knew everything about working, construction, electrical, education but discovered I knew little to nothing about women. The little I knew I had heard at the local gin mill or hanging out with the boys. Obviously, they did not know too much either. Men need to know more than the fact that women are made physically different from them.

Women walked me through the lovemaking process teaching me to be sensitive to their needs, to slow down, respect female intuition so I could enjoy her complete richness.

They taught me that making love to a woman is more than simply satisfying a sexual appetite, that I should enjoy the gourmet buffet of sexual gratification. Did you know that soft words soothe a womans' countenance and strengthens her sensuality? Or that her gentle, passionate spirit reassures a mans confidence? The true love of a woman is boundless. Her grace is sweeter than warm Savannah honeysuckle and if you fully accept it you will believe that you can conquer the world. I mean, you really believe there is nothing that you cannot achieve.

HOWARD N. HUNTER

From her softness, I learned to confront and deal with life's issues without anxiety and depression. The only power struggle in the relationship was the one she had empowering me to be myself for my greater good.

Women are natural nurturers. They supported me as I matured. To all of the women who have graced my life in one way or the other—living or dead, good, bad or indifferent—beginning with my birth mother and my grandmother, I am eternally grateful. Men, when you fully respect women you will live long healthy enriching lives.

To my little brothers, the next time you're upset, open up to a good woman—not just any female—a woman. This is not weakness. It is a strength. You will not be disappointed but delightfully surprised.

I have fought the good fight and have been inspired toward deep intimacy and meaningful relationships. As a man I understand that real women are more precious than gold. They are finer than silver and nothing compares to her by your side. Through her strengths you will easily make your transition to manhood.

Chapter Fifteen

Still Reaching and Teaching

I HAVE BEEN YOUNG, and now I am old, yet I have not seen the righteous forsaken nor his seed begging bread said David the Psalmist. (Psalms 37:25). That is one of my favorite Bible passages.

It is no secret and most people who have known me for a moment know that I used to indulge in strong drink. As a matter of fact that is how some people still remember me today. They say, you mean Howard, the guy who drinks like a fish? I have come so far conquering and overcoming the mistakes of my life but not many people recognize those triumphs. They hold onto my mistakes, reminding me of them, using selective memory when it is convenient.

I began drinking as a man and I take full responsibility for my actions. The drinking caused me many of the same problems as it causes others. When I recognize some of the problems other brothers have encountered I am glad mine was one I could overcome despite the consequences.

This extracurricular activity landed me in a detoxification treatment center in Connecticut where I worked a program of recovery and I was doing very well. In rehab I was awaken to the biggest lie I ever told myself that I did not have a problem with alcohol. I definitely had a problem with alcohol. Telling myself that lie made it easier to lie to myself about other things. I learned to confront myself and live anew. This is what I learned about myself.

I was a high functioning alcoholic, able to perform most of life's sustainable tasks. I took care of myself, performed well at work, attended events, finished school, took care of my business, paid my bills and like most alcoholics told myself that I could stop drinking when I was ready to stop.

I did not become a recovering alcoholic until I and others stopped making excuses for the drinking. At that time I worked hard at it. The decision to stop drinking is one of the hardest ones that I ever had to make. It required that I completely reevaluate my life, as well as, my actions past and present. It was not an easy process and not something I would recommend anyone deals with alone. For sure I needed help kicking that alcohol habit.

Today, I am so grateful for that treatment facility and the steps of Alcoholics Anonymous. I am so glad for the groups' purpose to carry its' message to alcoholics that are still suffering. That was me! I was suffering and did not know it.

A counselor told my counseled group that I was in the bottom of the alcohol bottle. He explained to them that I had risen to the top through self-dedication, hard work, study, preparation and by fighting segregation, overcoming racism and single parentage to hold some of the most prestigious jobs in the country that had never been offered to other black men. That statement was a slap of sobering reality. Although I had lived it I had never thought about it like that. I thought, if I could do all of that I could stare down my personal demons and take control of my life again.

While in treatment I decided to stop drinking but it was going to take more than a decision to help me get and stay sober. I needed to make some serious changes, like strengthen my spiritual foundation and place principles before personalities. As I said before, this treatment facility and the opportunities it afforded me was the best thing that had happened to me in a very long time.

Living independently I have endured temptation by so called "friends" who were well aware of my personal struggles. Some refused to befriend me unless I engaged in strong drink with them. It's true misery loves company.

I was accepting some harsh realities and dealing with myself in the recovery center when a co-worker approached me with a strange question. He asked me if I had talked with the director of the alcohol recovery program where I was recovering. I told him I had not.

The next day the supervisor of the recovery program asked to speak with me privately. He explained that the recovery facility had a new program that they wanted to try out. The program offered participants, like myself, an opportunity to utilize their skills, gifts and talents in the community while stabilizing themselves in the recovery program. It would also keep participants grounded and focused in the community where they would eventually be mainstreamed.

The executives had held a meeting and decided that since I already had such a vibrant presence in the community I would be a great candidate to work the program.

The next day, I went to lunch with my co-workers. We discussed the program and I leaned more about it. The supervisor asked if the director of the program had talked to me. I told him that we had a long discussion. I was surprised when he showed me a paper signed by the Brigadier General of the facility specifically requesting my participation in this new program.

The request was for me to teach in the program two days a week! I was shocked but delighted to be considered. The terms of the agreement included two days a week excused absences from the program to teach Electrical Principals at Prince Technical High School in Hartford Connecticut. Of course I accepted. Every Tuesday and Thursday I was picked up from the rehab facility and taken to teach at Prince Tech. After class I stopped with the boys for a coffee or a snack and returned to the facility.

The security officers at the facility waved me in with looks of concern on their faces. I could tell they wondered what I was doing leaving the facility and returning at what looked like my leisure but they never had the nerve to ask me anything about what I was doing.

They did not know that I was making more money for teaching those two days a week than they were making for an entire month. I worked with the program until state funding for it was pulled from the education budget.

That program changed my life. I began to recognize my personal greatness and to see myself in a new, sharper perspective. I began to identify myself as a Certified Skills Educator, a Certified Pubic Accountant and an educated black man honorably discharged from the United States Marines and not as an alcoholic. The reflections in my life's mirror showed a vibrant person cross trained as an Electrician and a construction work. The real Howard surfaced. I returned to my community activism, a church representative, a youth leader and a stand-up kind of guy. The ashes of alcoholism returned me to a living, vibrant human being.

I had twenty-three students, twenty-two white and one black and a one hundred percent graduation rate that met all program requirements. Not at any time did my students know that they were being taught by a guy society had cast away. I doubt very much if many people have had this opportunity. We are not usually given this chance. Programs are not usually funded on the premise that a recovering alcoholic will be teaching the class.

In keeping with the premise of this book I wanted to share this personal success story in the hope that we may understand that alcoholism is not the person it is a disease much like many others that can be successfully treated.

Drinking to excess may or may not be a persons choice but it is a very serious disease that can and will ruin a life if not properly understood and treated. It may be passed from one generation to the next. Scientist are examining whether it is genetic. This is serious.

If alcoholism affects you or someone you love you may believe that the alcoholic simply lacks control. Many observers say things like "he" or "she" can stop drinking if they really want to or if they put their mind to it. Blaming cannot cure this disease. While simply having the desire to stop drinking may work for some a better way to start the recovery process is for the alcoholic to reach out for help to groups like Alcoholics Annonymous.

I have written this book because I want the reader to know it has always been felt that Blacks were not high achievers and that for some reason whites were somehow "smarter" than other races. And if for some reason they were alcoholics they really were considered ineffective. This is not true. Ones ability has little or nothing to do with the color of the skin of a person. When Blacks are relegated to subservient positions it may not be because they are only qualified for that position. The same with people who face challenges like alcoholism. Every man given a chance can surprise us with their abilities.

At the time of this writing I am proud to say that the playing field is beginning to level off. I am witnessing something I never thought would happen in my lifetime, a Black person is president of this free country.

Indeed the tide is turning but it will take a long time before the realities of what this country has suffered, due to its discriminating laws and policies, will be completely reversed. We have a long way to go.

When we discover the number of scientist, inventors, artists, teachers, politicians, writers who were not given a chance to express their genius we will understand why America has only advanced her society this far. Many of America's pieces of advanced civilization are buried in our local cemeteries and their genius has never been tapped because of the color of their skin.

Is it possible that America could have buried the cure for Cancer with a Black man? What about the cure for HIV? Could America have disallowed proper education to a black female researcher because she was female and black and therefore never discovered the cure for the common cold or Pneumonia? What can America have boast if she had allowed Black students into Harvard or Yale back in the day? Is it possible that America could still be the worlds superpower if she had effectually equalized the education of Black, Brown and White children? We will never know the injustices America has heaped upon her own head due to her racial injustices and internal ignorances.

Most of us know the story of Benjamin Banneker, that he was an astronomer, clock maker, publisher and how he wrote almanacs. We are familiar with his genius that helped convince whites that blacks were not intellectually inferior. He is only one slave son that speaks to the intelligence of Black people throughout Americas history.

According to records kept by the White House Historical Association, slaves and freed slaves often worked seven days a week in the hot and humid summers when noone else would. A list of construction workers building the white house in 1795 includes five slaves named Tom, Peter, Ben, Harry and Daniel all put to work as carpenters.

Other slaves worked as masons in the government quarries, cutting the stone for early government buildings, including the White House and the U.S. Capitol. Acting in her right mind what else could America have built?

With the browning of America it would be the height of ignorance for her to continue the farce of racism. If black and brown do not continue to build this country, who will?

The next time you witness injustices being perpetrated upon someone because of the color of their skin ask yourself if they could hold the cure for a disease that have not yet been discovered.

HOWARD N. HUNTER

Chapter Sixteen

Never Stop Achieving

I CONSIDERED THE LIFETIME Achievement Award as one of the finest awards of recognition. I would have probably been just another black man who made significant contributions to the world without acknowledgment, had it not been for a good friend of mine who saw the value of those contributions to the world.

Colleen Cyr is the research historian of the Meriden Connecticut branch of the (NAACP), the National Association for the Advancement of Colored People. She is a tireless worker on behalf of blacks. During conversation, Colleen explained that she wanted to recommend me for the Connecticut's African-American Affairs Commission Lifetime Achievement Award. I was shocked, not at Colleen, but that she thought my contributions were worthy and significant enough to mention, much less to qualify me for such a prestigious award.

After a few interviews, Colleen wrote the biography of my life that made this grown man cry. In it she included many of my achievements including being a pioneer and instrumental in breaking down the walls of segregation in the United States Marines.

She mentioned my membership in the Marine Corps League; first black New England officer of the New England Boy Scouts, Marine Corps League; first black Past Perfect President of the Local Lions Club District 23B; judge and chairman of (VICA); the Vocational Industrial Clubs of America, founding member and chairman of Each One-Teach One Inc., (CT) a youth personal development organization in Bloomfield, CT.; first black elected president of Connecticut's New Britain Veterans Council; first black vice-chair commissioner of the Local Inland Wetlands Commission of Bloomfield, Connecticut, first black New England instructor for (IBEW) (Local #35); International Brotherhood of Electrical Workers. I authored the article "We Must

Save Tomorrow, but First We Must Save Today" which is translated into seventeen languages through the International Lions Club.

I told Colleen that I thought this award recognized people who had achieved something in their lives. I believed that I had offered no significance to society. It was only when someone of Colleen's qualifications recognized it that I felt a real sense of worth.

I heard that when baby elephants are born, trainers place a huge ball and chain around their neck. Wherever the baby elephants walked they pulled that heavy chain with them. When the elephants were six months old, the trainers replace the chain with a long piece of kite twine but the elephants' reaction to that perceived weight around their neck did not change.

They struggled against what they believed was the heavy chain failing to make the mental adjustment to the lighter weighted twine. They had mentally and physically conditioned themselves to the heavier weighted chain.

Observers monitoring the elephants wondered why the huge, now adult elephants, would not allow themselves to go further than the tug of the length of that tiny string. They concluded that the elephant began life with a huge chain around thier neck. They grew accustomed to the weight of the heavy chain. No matter the weight of the thin string around their neck they still believed the task would be either too difficult to achieve or the energy needed to move it would not be worth the fight. So they gave up without trying.

It would not be until the elephants realized that the string was no longer the heavy chain that they would believe that the task may be achievable.

It is the same way with blacks in America today. We have carried the weight of racism, segregation, and discrimination for a very long time. It will take some time to realize the load is getting lighter and we can achieve our personal goals.

As the first African-American Electrical Skill instructor in New England, I have written practical, formal, and theoretical logistics of Electrical Education. I have designed a formal Electrical Skill Curriculum to advance electrical education. I have had my professional licence for thirty-four years and taught in America's high schools and finer trade schools providing some of the finest electricians in this country and abroad. Many have probably wired your homes and

HOWARD N. HUNTER

businesses. Yet, I questioned whether I could qualify for that Lifetime Achievement Award. It was the weight of the initial chain I was still dealing with. I realize now that it is only a string and I can move freely with it to achieve my goals.

Students receive me warmly. Their parents express gratitude for the impact they say I have made on their personal lives and families. They point out that thier children's self-esteem increased and thier families are intact due to my mentoring, teaching, and encouragement.

I am grateful to have made such positive impacts on the lives of these young people and hope they will use their greatness as a force for the betterment of America.

However, Colleen felt my contributions were significant and it was time I was recognized for them. She made the recommendation. In 2008, I received the Lifetime Achievement Award from The local African-American Affairs Commission.

He Who Has a Trade

Benjamin Franklin said "He, who has a trade, has an estate." That is a true statement. After leaving the military, I needed employment that could sustain me. I also wanted to do something to help others in the process. After long thought and other ventures failed, I decided I needed a trade. I returned to trade school and became an electrician.

My job was to ensure public safety. That meant learning and following the state and local building and national electrical codes. I learned to read blueprints, technical diagrams of circuits, outlets, load centers, and panel boards.

The first year I learned everything they put in front of me. I read, figured calculations and connected wires, circuit breakers, transformers, and outlets.

Becoming an electrician was a huge responsibility. Installing and maintaining wiring, adjusting fuses, and other components and maintaining electrical machines in factories was huge.

I was always a short guy, but when installing wires I felt taller than life. Using ammeters, ohmmeters, voltmeters, and oscilloscopes was exciting. I had been told all my life by society that no black man had ever amounted to anything, and I was no exception.

I focused on and mastered construction and maintenance work, fixing, upgrading existing systems, but I loved construction. I felt strong and in control.

Determining the diameter and number of wires installed depended upon me understanding how much power would be needed to run through it. That's good stuff! Just talking about it makes me want to pull out my old blueprints and create something interesting.

There was and still is a sense of personal gratification and pride when I pass by buildings that I personally wired and or piped in walls following blueprints. Something wonderful happened inside of me when I made small pieces come together, flipped a switch, and the lights came on or the motor started.

From the professionals, I learned about coaxial and fiber optics and how to correct problems before they became a problem.

I worked with homeowners rewiring and replacing old fuse boxes with newer technology to accommodate new appliances. The professionals taught me the skill, but helping regular people sparked something inside of me—seeing the joy on their faces when I helped them resolve a problem they thought to be unsolvable. I just loved construction.

I worked long hours inside and outside on strenuous jobs and lifting heavy objects. Forty hours was a standard work week but overtime was required. I never passed up overtime, including nights and weekends and was always on call to go to the next worksite. Sometimes I worked back to back shifts. I loved the long dollars that came with it.

Although personal injury was a constant threat, I trusted the knowledge of the strict safety rules and practices to keep me safe as I applied them.

The industry was a vast platform of education. I advised management on hazardous equipment, consulted with engineers and technicians, line installers, and maintenance workers.

In the apprentice program I was pulling good money. I was a member of the Brotherhood Program of Electrical Workers, local chapter of Electrical Contractors Association. I had access to unlimited opportunities and I took advantage of every one of them. I took every class available to help me improve my job. I was mentored by experienced electricians and became proficient in every area of electrical tasks.

The apprenticeship program afforded me the opportunity to start employment at an advanced salary and experience level than those without the apprenticeship training.

By the time I was on a job, I knew how to set a job site up and gather materials. I was a high school graduate having received my GED in the marines. I continued company specific safety trainings in management and contract law.

Licensed

I took the licensure test on Electrical Theory, the National Electrical Code, and local electric and building codes and passed it the first time with flying colors. I continued with union and employer courses to learn about changes in the National Electrical Code.

I wanted to become an electrical contractor and needed the special Master Electrician License. Connecticut required me to have at least three years of experience as an electrician. I already had it! I took the test and today I am a Master Electrician.

A requirement to become an electrician meant that I had to have great manual dexterity, eye-hand coordination, and be physically fit with a good sense of balance. I also needed good color vision to be able to identify electrical wires by color. My good work history and military service looked favorable. I had both a good work history and an honorable discharge from the marines.

I was promoted to supervisory position, became a project manager and a site supervisor. With this job came sufficient capital management skills and wanted to start my own contracting business. This venture would require two special contractors and I would assume the supervisory job in the interim.

I was ready. I knew the job. I did not want to go into the business alone and I needed another type of business license. I asked a "friend" who had the other license necessary. I tried to convince him to come along by showing him where we could go with the business. We talked and talked but he could not see the vision.

It soon became a reality that our visions for success were very different and I gave up the idea. I learned from that experience that friends or others may or may not share your personal vision but you are never to give up. The only person who needed to see that vision was me.

I needed to keep talking until I found a business partner who did share the vision. I had to ask myself if my friend was willing to invest his potential in my idea. I should have realized that after all of that begging he was just not interested, but it was not for me to give up on my own idea. I needed to pursue another business partner who would be able to see my point of view or at least help me see theirs. I had gone the distance and I lost.

I recommend the skill of electrical. It is a growing industry and is expected to increase as fast as the average for all occupations.

As America increases her use of Green Technology, more electricians will be needed. President Barack Obama has plans to rebuild bridges and schools across this nation. New buildings will need new wiring for computers and telecommunications equipment. Robots and other automated manufacturing systems in factories also will require the installation and maintenance of more complex wiring systems.

In addition, increased demand for electrical work will be expected over the next decade as a large number of electricians retire. This creates excellent job opportunities, especially for those of you with the widest range of skills, including voice, data and video wiring.

Job openings for electricians vary by location and specialty, however, and will be best in the fastest growing part of the country, especially those areas where power plants are being constructed. Be ready to travel to the big money.

No Excuse for Poverty

I have told you throughout this book that Sarah did not allow me to use words like "can't" and "sorry." There were no excuses that she allowed me to have. Likewise, there is no excuse for you to live in and claim poverty either. So you are not the best in all subjects in school. No excuse. Study. No high school diploma. Get one! No excuses accepted on the road to your success. Change your excuses into obstacles you need to overcome. Set goals. Reach one. Set another.

I talk about electrical here because it worked for me. You can choose a trade that you like. They are all excellent. I asked a friend of mine why he wanted to become a plumber. It did not seem to me to be the most attractive trade. He told me he could become a brain surgeon but if the water did not run in the sink, he would not be able to do his job. In fact, being called to the emergency room for a surgery and he could not take a shower, he could not do his job. Made sense to him and after he explained it made sense to me too. All trades are excellent and all will keep you and your family off of the welfare roles.

Invest in yourself and your education. You are worth it. Get the appropriate licenses and certifications. Do as well as you can in high school so you can pass any assessment test. If you are in high school you can gain credits toward apprenticeship training under Registered Apprenticeship Programs. Take rigorous high school courses in math and physics. Do well in applied math and science.

Become a journeyman. Get a journeyman's certificate. Study and pass entrance level competence exams. Find a suitable employer who is willing to hire and train you. Most employers prefer to hire and train an apprentice. Get that apprenticeship!

Keep your nose clean. Keep the law on the right side of you. I can tell you stories of people who lived their lives clean and made one simple mistake that cost them their full ability to live like they wanted to live.

Sometimes as youngsters we think that a crime committed as a juvenile will be swept under the rug. Be careful what you think may be a misdemeanor can come back to bite you in the behind. Sometimes laws change and that misdemeanor can become a felony without you knowing it. If that happens, you will have a bigger problem getting what you want in life. Although laws are being written to support people who have felonies, you do not want to find yourself in that trap. Keep your nose clean. It's your life. It's your journey. Make the best of it!

Chapter Seventeen

Born Again
The Eighth Wonder

I HAVE A SHORT personal story I want to share with you about my love for electricity. After mastering the National Electrical program my skills quality was second to none. I accepted employment with the union and worked as a crew member building the brand new Buckland Hills Mall in Manchester, Connecticut. I was doing well and everything seemed to be going fine. My life seemed to be on course and I had even started some spiritual soul searching as I do often.

Remnants of the recent holidays were still quite evident. I had gone to church and was feeling quite well about myself. The service had been encouraging and I was experiencing personal renewal.

Tuesday, January 9, 1990, was an extremely cold day in Connecticut. Old man winter had promised Connecticut a huge snow storm including six to nine inches of snow but delivered only a drifting white powder.

I was the electrical foreman on the construction crew building the mall. There were several men on this crew including my apprentice. The mall was nearing completion and one of the major commercial vendors pushed to have their electrical work finished earlier than projected. In fact, they wanted the lightning working by that night. We worked to meet the evening deadline.

The crew finished our morning coffee break as we walked back to our designated sites. All things seemed normal—we were jesting and joking about life in general but my life was about to change.

As the working foreman, I went to work quickly to get the circuit lights working. I mounted the engine power lift and signaled to the ground crew to raise the power lift rig.

Once up, I noticed the coil wires were tangled and extremely warm. I needed to untangle them. I signaled the ground crew to lower the power lift. They lowered me to the ground to get some materials and lifted again. Besides the warmth of the coils, nothing seemed unusual. I assumed they were grounded as it was standard practice that they would be grounded. I reached for the coils and my body became energized with electrical current. I could not speak. I could not breathe and felt as if I was losing oxygen.

I heard a piercing sound as a rushing freight train moving at the speed of lightning. Everything I had ever done in life was flying past me like a movie on fast-forward and going in the opposite direction. I saw it and understood it all. I was not moving.

As a child, I had been hit in my right eye with a huge rock and the trauma rendered me nearly blind in that eye. Suddenly my visual acuity was clear as the hope diamond and I could see the distance like a hawk in the wind. My body sashayed like a feather and ascended like a rocket. Every thought was crystallized as they faded to reflections. These changes happened between the time the electricity hit me and at that time I hit the ground.

Although the right side of my body was on fire I felt no pain. My breath was undetectable and leaving me at a snail's pace. My pulse was weak, muscles contracting and my body had become rigid and still. In a weird sense, I knew this was happening, but I could feel nothing. My body slowly melded with the universe. I had often been teased as the shortest guy in any crowd with friends asking me if I was standing up when they knew good and well I was standing up. But now I was as tall as the highest heavens, unanchored, high-ranking, and soaring in the wind. What a feeling! I was in a place of dignity and beauty, and I was forever changed.

I had been hit by 480 volts of electricity, and my heart had stopped. In the process, I heard, not saw, the infamous light. It was so bright that it rang in my ears. I could literally hear the light! It illuminated every cell in my body and held me in its grip. I was one with an energy source that I had never known. Where did I end, and where did that energy begin?

As I relate this story, my memory is pregnant with images of men and women that I had met in the marines. They looked like smoking chimneys.

Familiar street names, tall buildings, and highways that I had traveled as a child in Savannah were in living color. Conversations with my grandmother were personified and stood as "truths" beckoning me to come to them.

Suddenly, I couldn't breathe, and I raced into a dark tunnel. There was a brighter light amid the brightness, and the darkness disappeared. For some odd reason and in that moment, I understood that darkness did not comprehend light. The darkness disappeared. I became part of that smooth brilliance.

On the other side of that brilliance stood a round, full moon shaped light, brighter than any light I had ever seen. It had a familiar smell—like the smell of love in my grandmother's arm that I smelled when I had been born in Savannah. In a strange sense it was sweeter than Sarah's love. There were loud crashing sounds in the background reminding me of the two years I spent back and forth in the hospital overcoming polio and learning how to walk again. Was it my grandmother's love that she shared with me so many times? Was it the gentleness and goodness of Aunt Laura's different kind of love? No. It was all of that and so much more. I was convinced that there could be no greater love than this.

The light of this love covered the bigotry, prejudice, injustice, discrimination, and inequalities that I had ever experienced. My mind burst with the knowledge that I had not lived a perfect life myself.

I arrived at Manchester Memorial Hospital where they ran a complete battery of tests including EKG, ECG for muscle enzymes and significant muscle injury. They scanned my body for fractures, dislocations, and broken bones. Many parts of my body had been broken. Full side stapling was required on my right side. The bones had to be stabilized with metal. I still have that metal holding my body together today.

I awoke after two days in a coma and hours and hours of extensive surgery. The pain was unbearable. I was in terrible pain. The damaged, withered, and atrophied muscles in my right side had been removed and replaced with metal rods and there were no promises.

No one was making any promises as to if I would walk again, nor could they tell me the level of recovery that I could expect, if any. It was in this time I heard Sarah exclaim, "You will walk!" I had been at this juncture before. Sarah declared that I would walk back then and I declared I would walk again.

Would it be a struggle? Yes. But I was use to struggle. From the time I pushed myself through that black tunnel to be born, I was a survivor. This recovery would be a piece of cake.

Limb amputations had been seriously considered but by the Grace of God, the skill of a master surgeon, and the best doctors in the region most of my limbs had been spared. My heart and other vital internal organs had been affected to varying degrees, but not totally destroyed. Thanks to the fast action of the medical community most had been spared major damage.

How could that be? Medical observers said my blood fluctuated between freezing and boiling from zero degrees Celsius to 212 degrees Fahrenheit.

The doctors and nurses stood by my bed with a story like no other. None of them had expected me to pull through, and in fact most had given me up to die. The nurses marveled as they explained how the electricity had seared my bones and melted my flesh like melting cheese. They told me I was in very bad shape. They explained that this was an indication of things to expect in my recovery, if there was going to be a recovery.

I felt a huge childlike appreciation. Everyone expected me to take the turn for the worst. They even called my minister, the Rev. King T. Hayes to deliver my last rites. But I was unbelievably blessed. There was no permanent brain damage and no sign of seizure disorders. In that moment I realized the old Howard was gone and truly I had been born again.

If there had ever been an unlucky place to be at the time of that accident, it was in that lift. I was at the worst possible place at the worst possible time. Think about this: I was at the highest point from the safety of the ground. I was in the air without shelter wearing a watch and waist tool belt with metal buckles and tools attached! A metal crane hugged me and I was standing on a metal platform.

Since electricity naturally seeks the fastest path to the ground it moved like lightning through my entire body searching for an exit.

Electricity burns from the inside out and my body was indeed a towering inferno. The doctors poked and prodded, turned, rolled, and lifted me searching for external injuries besides the obvious.

Many of my injuries could be seen with the naked eye, others required exploratory examinations. My skin was burnt red and severely charred having lost two shades of my natural skin color.

I asked Doctor Passaretti if I was going to make it. He looked at me with a compassionate stare and in an unforgettable tone reassured me hesitantly that I was going to make it.

After that experience I was a changed man. When I came out of that coma I was a brand new me and I would never be the same. My personality changed for the better and that was a good thing.

You see, before that experience I had a foul, potty mouth. I wasn't a sailor but I could deliver a ringer better than the next guy. I was an angry man. I felt like I had paid my dues and been unfairly treated by society.

I had spent years trying to do the right thing only to be rejected by my fellow man. My priorities had gotten crossed. I believed in ignorant stereotypes. Some were better than others, the lighter the skin the better the stereotype. And as if it mattered, I believed that my curly hair was like white people's hair, because it was not nappy like my black brothers' hair. My hair needed only water or baby oil to make it lay flat down on my head.

I was at least two shades lighter than the average black person and I had blue eyes. I took pride in the fact that everyone noticed this black man with blue eyes.

I thought I was the man. Upon reflection I realized that I had been just as prejudice and discriminatory as some of my fairer-skinned brothers. Not that it makes a difference, but they are white. I am not and was rudely awakened when a white brother reminded me that I was not a white man.

I lived by the creed that construction workers could drink alcohol by the volumes. I was a construction worker and I took pride in the fact that I could drink the best guy under the table. I was proud and boasted that I made the big money to buy the best and I drank only from the top shelf.

I would let a woman know in a minute that I was not begging, I was buying and paying top dollar if she was interested.

I had served my country through the United States Marines and been denied the opportunity to be an officer because of the color or my skin.

HOWARD N. HUNTER

I had tried the traditional route of marriage and family and failed to get satisfaction from those hard-fought relationships.

I had used my talents to teach children and adults and struggled to live by society's guidelines. Yet I was constantly annoyed and easily provoked. I was always heated!

The electrocution strengthened my resolve about life. Today, I respect myself and hold others in due high regard no matter the color of their skin. I use words carefully to strengthen my weaknesses. I recognize that life is about people, not pursuits. It is about love, not hate; about faith, not fate. It is the small act of unconditional love that comes to any man. Today, I hardly give thought to the drink. Indulgence in it takes sound thought and critical choice.

I was sent home to my nine-room house to recuperate. I was trapped in my recreation room for six months. As a result, I have renewed appreciation for other people. I respect others' accomplishments.

Although my fridge was full of food on the first floor I could not get to it. Suddenly, if I could get off of my crutches, going to the grocery store would not be an imposition. As a matter of fact, I would have given anything to be able to do that myself.

I had three completely furnished bedrooms and could not sleep in either of them as they were on the second floor; three bathrooms and could only access the sink in the basement. My closets were filled with new suits and shoes and I wore the same clothes day after day.

Whenever I opened the garage door I was reminded that I owned a custom van and an automobile but couldn't drive either one.

I learned to not complain when I had to make an extra effort to go somewhere, but to be thankful that I was able to go and had been blessed with the transportation to travel in.

I lived in the recreation room because it was the most convenient place. You see, I had to open the garage door for the Meals on Wheels Food Program serving the needs of homebound people. I would open the garage door and they would stick a couple of white boxes of food inside to me. I learned to be grateful when I could fix my own food and to have compassion on those who could not.

I remained a prisoner in my own home unable to walk up or down my own stairs. Considering these consequences I decided to walk in a new life. I had to renew my thinking.

As I reflect on my terrible condition I realize how truly blessed I am. Although I could not get up to any other floors of the house, I was forced to appreciate the fact that I still had a house and my basic needs were met.

I was alone in the recreation room counting the wall panels and my cousin came to help me. He stayed a while, helped me pay the bills, and cleaned the area where I lived. I was really glad to have him with me. He literally became my right hand. Family matters. I learned to never take them for granted. When it is just you, you had better be able to depend on someone.

It does not matter where you go in life or how you get there; but if you are going to be successful in life, remember to never look down on anyone unless you are reaching to pick them up.

For anyone who questions the legitimacy of this story, I have enclosed the original Report of Operation from Manchester Memorial Hospital in Manchester, Connecticut, where I was rushed from the construction site. I encourage anyone to read this report. I would appreciate your thoughts and comments about any part of my writings. Send them to me at *Hunter.Howard@sbcglobal.net.*

ßW

NAME: HUNTER, Howard
ACCT/HIST #: 589-847
MR #: 04-67-30

REPORT OF OPERATION

1/10/90   2,000 - 2,500 cc

Michael Passaretti, M.D.

Preoperative Diagnosis: Spiral fracture proximal shaft of right
                               femur.

Postoperative Diagnosis: Spiral fracture proximal shaft of right
                               femur.

Operation: Open reduction, internal fixation using
                               lag screw and interfragmentary screws.

After satisfactory induction of a general endotracheal anesthesia, the patient was positioned on the fracture table. Using image intensification the fracture was reduced. The patient was then prepped and draped in the usual sterile manner. A lateral skin incision was made and carried through the skin and subcutaneous tissue. The fascia lata was divided. The vastus lateralis muscle fascia was divided and the muscle was split in the posterior one third to expose the shaft of the femur. Copious bleeding was encountered and this was controlled with clamps and electrocoagulation. The fracture was identified. It was a long spiral fracture beginning at the lesser trochanteric area and extending to the junction of the middle and distal one-third of the femur. The head and neck of the femur were attached to the proximal fracture fragment laterally and the distal shaft was attached to the medial spiral fracture proximally. Using manipulation and direct manipulation the fracture was reduced and held reduced with Lowman clamps. Excellent reduction was achieved. With image intensification control a Kirschner wire was then placed through a drill hole made in the distal shaft of the femur into the head and neck at a 135 degree angle. This was then reamed and tapped and an 80 mm lag screw was then introduced into the head and neck of the femur. A 135 standard barrel 14-hole side-plate was then placed under the lag bolt and beneath the Lowman clamps with the fracture site anatomically reduced. A compression knot was then applied. The screws were then placed into the plate and two interfragmentary screws placed anteriorly through the fracture site directly. Excellent fixation and reduction were achieved. The wound was then copiously and thoroughly irrigated. Hemovac drain was inserted. The wound was then closed in interrupted layers.

CONTINUED...

Original page 1 hospital report

~~Dummary : 0~~ ~~.....~~

MANCHESTER MEMORIAL HOSPITAL
MANCHESTER, CONNECTICUT

NAME: HUNTER, Howard
ACCT/HIST #: 589-847
MR #: 04-67-30

REPORT OF OPERATION   Page 2

The estimated blood loss is between 2,000 and 2,500 cc.
patient received four units of blood during the procedure.

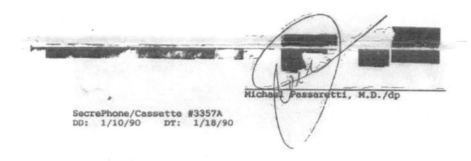

Michael Passaretti, M.D./dp

SecrePhone/Cassette #3357A
DD: 1/10/90   DT: 1/18/90

Original 2 page hospital report

Chapter Eighteen

The Giant Within

A FEW YEARS AGO, I sat down to review and replace some old values that no longer served me well and to make a conscious decision to change a few things in my life. As I journey through life I will continue to review and make changes for the better. Today, I am living well.

I was recently saddened by the death of my aunt who had been a very important member of my family with whom I grew up. This lady had more friends than anyone I had ever known. Although I visited often and celebrated with her on her 107th, 108th, and 109th birthdays, I believe I fell short on showing my real appreciation to her place in this world.

The Baptist church that held her home-going ceremony acknowledged grandchildren, great-grandchildren, and great-great-grandchildren who were all dressed in white in her honor. They told of her greatness and celebrated her life. It was beautiful to hear the hearts and lives she had touched in such a short one hundred and nine years.

This book is included in the new approach to live my life to the fullest, away with superficial relationships and future regrets. I left them all in yesterday. Tomorrow is not guaranteed to me. If I live until tomorrow, I will count it all God's grace. But today is the present. The present is a gift. That is why it is called the present. It gives me a chance to make tomorrow count for something. When you are tired, disappointed, or feeling cheated, choose to live your life in the present. Live it to the fullest moment every day.

Make amends to people you have hurt. Don't practice ignorance or refuse to apologize for your shortcomings. Don't make it difficult for someone to approach you. Let go of arrogant behavior. Live as if you are dying. The fact is that from the time we are born, we begin the dying process. There is no time to waste living a great life.

The program *American's Most Wanted* ends its weekly broadcast with a very fitting tribute to officers who died in the line of duty and I paraphrase, "It is not how they died that makes them great. It is how they lived." Don't let your death be more celebrated than your life.

Become a "No Matter What" Person

Auntie was a "no matter what" person. She held her core values close to her breast and dared not waiver them. In the face of cowardice she bravely confronted her fears. She stood her ground to overcome objections. I learned from her and you can learn from me.

At Auntie's funeral I heard a gospel song that stirred my soul, "Let the Works I've Done Speak for me." It has deeply changed my life for the better. Take a listen. It will change you.

A Letter to the World's Children

Dear Children:

I have written *"Tenure"* in the hope that it will positively charge you to take control of your lives. I challenge you not to allow your personal circumstances to become your life's hindrance, rather appoint them as stepping stones to your personal greatness.

Tenure is designed to give you tools to endure life's turbulence. I walk with you through the difficult times of my life to prove to you that nothing is impossible when you set your goals high enough, develop good character, and test on solid integrity you can boldly live your life.

You will never be too young or too old to overcome a challenge. Many people wait for solutions to come to them. Solutions will not come to them, and none will come to you either. You must grab life by the throat and demand of it what is in it for you. You can make it happen sooner or later. The longer you wait the more difficult challenges are to overcome.

Engage in self-learning. Consistently evaluate all circumstances and decisions. Recommit to being your best and your life will be fulfilled. I remain dedicated to all of your successes in life.

Semper Fidelis

Epilogue

The Wonder of It All

EVER LEAVE A small child alone and return to wonder how he got out of that crib? This is the story of the Africans in America. We arrived on these shores with stolen identities and were forced to create new ones. Africans are the only group of people brought to this country against our free will. All other immigrants came to America looking for freedom, fairness, and greener pastures. Under dire circumstances, we overcame horrendous living conditions to carve out better lives for ourselves and our families.

We were stripped naked of our natural culture. We had no employment and were dependent upon the very captives who enslaved us for our most basic survival. We planted, harvested, tilled, and forced the ground to bear without benefit to us.

We wept as we bore mulatto children of the slave master and watched him sell them for his financial gain to our personal despair that we would never be able to identify or see our children again.

We built the White House, developed a new language, endured integration to the agony of personal separation. We lived in overcrowded cities and worked for menial compensation including minimum wage with few to no benefits.

More African Americans have died from strokes, heart disease, cancer, ulcers, and diabetes than any other group in America. We have fought battles across color and fear lines emerging victoriously, finding strength in each others' weaknesses.

Weary, worn, and slaughtered we climbed the mountains and trod stony ground on bare feet. We have agonized against the chastening rod. Before hope Gods' Grace was sufficient. We prayed for mercy and hope and truth delivered us. We encouraged each other. Our spirits bent but they never broke. Today we stand tall and accept a new beauty.

In the midst of a failing education system we have studied and graduated. We have withstood severe and unusual punishment to become disciplined. Although we were hated we have learned to love again.

We acknowledged and sought God. He has ordered our steps and directed our paths. As we move forward to new generations of accomplishments, we walk by faith.

So go forth, sons and daughters of Africa. Fulfill your God-given abilities. Let no one wrestle your greatness from you. Become the next baritones and tenors! The cures for cancer and AIDS are within the greatness of your minds. Molds for new hearts and lungs are being created in the strength of your hands. Sons, daughters, write your books and deliver yourselves. Remember that God is the only thing greater than yourself. It has been my pleasure to walk with you where there was no path and leave for you a magnificent trail.

Semper Fidelis!

HOWARD N. HUNTER

Suggested Readings

- Du Bois, W. E. B. *The Souls of Black Folk*. New York: Library of America, 1903.
- Kelly, Robin D. G. *Race Rebels: Culture, Politics, and the Black Working Class*. New York: Free Press, 1994.
- Lawrence Levine. *Black Culture and Black Consciousness: Afro-American Folk Thought from Slavery to Freedom*. New York: Oxford University Press, 1977.
- Scott, Daryl. *Contempt and Pity: Social Policy and Image of the Damaged Black Psyche, 1880-1996*. Chapel Hill: University of North Carolina Press, 1997.
- **Web References**: w*ww.pbs.org/wgbh/pages/frontline/shows/jefferson/mixed* w*ww.mixedheritagecenter.org/index.php?Itemid=29&id=1342&option=com_content&task=view* *www.jimcrowhistory.org/resources/lessonplans/hs_es_***passing_for_white**.*htm—21k—www.websitetoolbox.com/tool/post/mulattodebate/vpost?id=3138511—37k—www.ferris.edu/***jimcrow***/what.*htm—24k h*ttp//www.nps.gov/malu/documents/jim* crowlaws. htm.

A Lifetime of Achievement

Education

Certified Professional Educator (Related Courses) 98
Certified Professional Educator (Electrical) 90
Connecticut Master Electrical License
Albert I Prince Technical School, Electrical Certificate

Electrical Experience

Electrical/Electronics, Bloomfield High School
Electrical/Vinal Satellite School
Electrical Union Local #35 Senior Apprentice Instructor
Evening Instructor, Supplemental and State Program,
Albert I Prince Technical School
Union Electrician IBEW Hartford Local 35, 1967-1993
Millstone Nuclear Power Plant 1974-1981, Waterford, CT
Electrical Foreman, Thames Co-Generation Plant PEI, Electrical Contractors

Professional Oration Experience

Orator, Eagle Scout Honor Court, Hardware City Detachment, New Britain, CT exclusively: Farmington, Avon, Unionville, Canton, Bristol & New Canaan, CT
Youth Spokesperson Boy Scouts Sunday, Windsor, CT
School Military Patriotism Spokesperson, History/U.S. Flag Veteran's Day Spokesperson
Educational Advocate: Children, Youth, & Adults, Htfd, CT
James H. Moran Middle School, Wallingford, CT
Career Day Speaker, Electrical/ Electronic/Tech. Skills, 2004
Keynote Speaker, Career Day, Moran Middle School, 2005
Speaker: "Black History" U.S. M.C (1942-1949), Avon, CT

Achievements

Integrated U.S. Marine Corps (1949-1952), Honorable Discharge
U.S. Marine Corps Boot Camp, Integrated Platoon
Excelsior Masonic Lodge#3 (PHA) Hartford, CT
Royal Arch Chapter (PHA) Hartford, CT

Past President and Chaplain, Bloomfield Lions Club
East Windsor Sportsman's Club, National Rifle Association
Lifetime Achievement Award: African-American Affairs Commission, CT

Honorable Distinction—Firsts

Senior Apprenticeship Instruction, New England District 3 International Brotherhood of Electrical, Local#35
Electrical Instructor, Albert I Prince Technical School, CT
US Postal Service: Building Trades Employee, CT

President, New Britain Veterans Council, CT
Boy Scout Youth Director, New England Division
Building Trade Instructor Vocational/Technical, CT
Super Star Substitute Award: Kelly Educational Services, CT

Community Outreach

Four distinguished Service Awards—Detachment, State of CT
Wake Detail-Detachment, Youth Activities, Marine Corp League
New England Division, Boy Scout, Liaison, present
Connecticut Public TV—Montford Point, Marines/Integration
Youth Outreach Chairman, Lions, Cabinet District—23B
Inland Wetland Watercourse
Commissioner, Bloomfield, CT
Educator's Workshop, Parris Island, South Carolina
Judge U.S. Skill Olympics, 1989, IBEW Washington, DC
Connecticut Electrical Chairperson,
Vocational Industrial Clubs of America (VICA)
Youth Activity Chair, Marine Corp League New Britain, CT
Eagle Scout Court of Honor, New England Div. Marine Corp League
Grand Marshall, Memorial Day Parade, Bloomfield, CT 2006
Justice of the Peace, Bloomfield, CT

Edwards Brothers, Inc.
Thorofare, NJ USA
May 20, 2011